2/05

D0385940

The Right
to Privacy

POINT COUNTERPOINT

Capital Punishment
Freedom of Speech
Gun Control
Mental Health Reform
The Right to Privacy
Trial of Juveniles as Adults

The Right to Privacy

Martha A. Bridegam, J.D.

SERIES CONSULTING EDITOR
Alan Marzilli, M.A., J.D.

CHELSEA HOUSE
P U B L I S H E R S
A Haights Cross Communications Company

Philadelphia

This book is intended to serve only as a general introduction to the political and legal issues surrounding the right to privacy. It is not intended as legal advice. If you have a legal problem, you should consult a licensed attorney who is familiar with the laws and procedures of your jurisdiction.

CHELSEA HOUSE PUBLISHERS

VP, NEW PRODUCT DEVELOPMENT Sally Cheney
DIRECTOR OF PRODUCTION Kim Shinners
CREATIVE MANAGER Takeshi Takahashi
MANUFACTURING MANAGER Diann Grasse

Staff for THE RIGHT TO PRIVACY

EDITOR Patrick M.N. Stone
PRODUCTION EDITOR Jaimie Winkler
PHOTO EDITOR Sarah Bloom
SERIES AND COVER DESIGNER Keith Trego
LAYOUT 21st Century Publishing and Communications, Inc.

A Haights Cross Communications ⚑ Company

http://www.chelseahouse.com

First Printing

1 3 5 7 9 8 6 4 2

Library of Congress Cataloging-in-Publication Data

Bridegam, Martha.
    The right to privacy/Martha Bridegam.
        p. cm.—(Point/counterpoint)
    Includes bibliographical references and index.
        ISBN 0-7910-7373-4 HC   0-7910-7508-7 PB
    1. Privacy, Right of—United States—Juvenile literature. [1. Privacy, Right of.]
    I. Title. II. Point-counterpoint (Philadelphia, Pa.)
    JC596.2.U5 B73 2002
    323.44'8'0973—dc21

                                                            2002152056

||||||||| CONTENTS

Introduction
Alan Marzilli, M.A., J.D.
Durham, North Carolina

The debates presented in POINT/COUNTERPOINT are among the most interesting and controversial in contemporary American society, but studying them is more than an academic activity. They affect every citizen; they are the issues that today's leaders debate and tomorrow's will decide. The reader may one day play a central role in resolving them.

Why study both sides of the debate? It's possible that the reader will not yet have formed any opinion at all on the subject of this volume—but this is unlikely. It is more likely that the reader will already hold an opinion, probably a strong one, and very probably one formed without full exposure to the arguments of the other side. It is rare to hear an argument presented in a balanced way, and it is easy to form an opinion on too little information; these books will help to fill in the informational gaps that can never be avoided. More important, though, is the practical function of the series: Skillful argumentation requires a thorough knowledge of *both* sides—though there are seldom only two, and only by knowing what an opponent is likely to assert can one form an articulate response.

Perhaps more important is that listening to the other side sometimes helps one to see an opponent's arguments in a more human way. For example, Sister Helen Prejean, one of the nation's most visible opponents of capital punishment, has been deeply affected by her interactions with the families of murder victims. Seeing the families' grief and pain, she understands much better why people support the death penalty, and she is able to carry out her advocacy with a greater sensitivity to the needs and beliefs of those who do not agree with her. Her relativism, in turn, lends credibility to her work. Dismissing the other side of the argument as totally without merit can be too easy—it is far more useful to understand the nature of the controversy and the reasons *why* the issue defies resolution.

The most controversial issues of all are often those that center on a constitutional right. The Bill of Rights—the first ten amendments to the U.S. Constitution—spells out some of the most fundamental rights that distinguish the governmental system of the United States from those that allow fewer (or other) freedoms. But the sparsely worded document is open to interpretation, and clauses of only a few words are often at the heart of national debates. The Bill of Rights was meant to protect individual liberties; but the needs of some individuals clash with those of society as a whole, and when this happens someone has to decide where to draw the line. Thus the Constitution becomes a battleground between the rights of individuals to do as they please and the responsibility of the government to protect its citizens. The First Amendment's guarantee of "freedom of speech," for example, leads to a number of difficult questions. Some forms of expression, such as burning an American flag, lead to public outrage—but nevertheless are said to be protected by the First Amendment. Other types of expression that most people find objectionable, such as sexually explicit material involving children, are not protected because they are considered harmful. The question is not only where to draw the line, but how to do this without infringing on the personal liberties on which the United States was built.

The Bill of Rights raises many other questions about individual rights and the societal "good." Is a prayer before a high school football game an "establishment of religion" prohibited by the First Amendment? Does the Second Amendment's promise of "the right to bear arms" include concealed handguns? Is stopping and frisking someone standing on a corner known to be frequented by drug dealers a form of "unreasonable search and seizure" in violation of the Fourth Amendment? Although the nine-member U.S. Supreme Court has the ultimate authority in interpreting the Constitution, its answers do not always satisfy the public. When a group of nine people—sometimes by a five-to-four vote—makes a decision that affects the lives of hundreds of millions, public outcry can be expected. And the composition of the Court does change over time, so even a landmark decision is not guaranteed to stand forever. The limits of constitutional protection are always in flux.

These issues make headlines, divide courts, and decide elections. They are the questions most worthy of national debate, and this series aims to cover them as thoroughly as possible. Each volume sets out some of the key arguments surrounding a particular issue, even some views that most people consider extreme or radical—but presents a balanced perspective on the issue. Excerpts from the relevant laws and judicial opinions and references to central concepts, source material, and advocacy groups help the reader to explore the issues even further and to read "the letter of the law" just as the legislatures and the courts have established it.

It may seem that some debates—such as those over capital punishment and abortion, debates with a strong moral component—will never be resolved. But American history offers numerous examples of controversies that once seemed insurmountable but now are effectively settled, even if only on the surface. Abolitionists met with widespread resistance to their efforts to end slavery, and the controversy over that issue threatened to cleave the nation in two; but today public debate over the merits of slavery would be unthinkable, though racial inequalities still plague the nation. Similarly unthinkable at one time was suffrage for women and minorities, but this is now a matter of course. Distributing information about contraception once was a crime. Societies change, and attitudes change, and new questions of social justice are raised constantly while the old ones fade into irrelevancy.

Whatever the root of the controversy, the books in POINT/COUNTERPOINT seek to explain to the reader the origins of the debate, the current state of the law, and the arguments on both sides. The goal of the series is to inform the reader about the issues facing not only American politicians, but all of the nation's citizens, and to encourage the reader to become more actively involved in resolving these debates, as a voter, a concerned citizen, a journalist, an activist, or an elected official. Democracy is based on education, and every voice counts—so every opinion must be an informed one.

In this volume, Martha Bridegam examines the sensitive issue of privacy, which has become especially controversial with the growing popularity of the Internet. Certain aspects of life are meant to be kept private—the home, diaries, medical conditions, relationships. Although the U.S. Constitution does not specifically mention "privacy," the right to privacy was a motivating factor in the American Revolution and has become a cornerstone of American law. But how much privacy do American citizens really have today?

The author examines some of the reasons why the right to privacy is so important to a free society. She also examines some of the possible justifications for infringing on privacy, including public safety and the public's "right to know."

Defining and Valuing the Right to Privacy

The right to privacy has become a hair-raisingly interesting topic. The world's laws and cultures are frantically adjusting to the implications of new technologies that can invade more or less anyone's privacy. Some of the most urgent controversies in the United States now have to do with drawing lines to protect individual privacy against unfair uses of new technologies. At the same time, the terrorist attacks of 2001 have renewed the perennial question of whether national crises justify increased government intrusion on personal privacy.

Which is more important—preserving the Bill of Rights or preserving national security?

Indignation against abusive government searches of private homes was one of the motivating forces behind the American

Revolution. However, the law of the United States has spelled out a legal right to privacy only relatively recently.

The Constitutional Basis

Congress and the states adopted the Constitution in 1789 and the Bill of Rights—the first ten Constitutional Amendments—in 1791. These founding documents added English borrowings to American innovations and spelled out an idea only implied in English law: that the people always retain a fundamental list of rights that no government action may violate. The Bill of Rights does not mention the word *privacy*, but it does restrain government interference in private life—through the First Amendment right to freedom of speech, religion, and association, the Fourth Amendment right against unreasonable searches and seizures, and the Fifth Amendment right to remain silent under official questioning.

The original Constitution accommodated slavery and denied women the right to vote, but through years of hard-fought amendment and interpretation it has come to offer near-equal formal rights to everyone in the United States.

Constitutional rights were interpreted to restrain only to federal laws and officials, not local officials such as police, until the 20th century, when the Bill of Rights was applied to state and local officials based on the "Due Process Clause" of the Fourteenth Amendment. (The Equal Protection and Due Process Clauses

THE LETTER OF THE LAW

The Fourth Amendment

The right of the people to be secure in their persons, houses, papers and effects, against unreasonable searches and seizures, shall not be violated, and no warrants shall issue, but upon probable cause, supported by oath or affirmation, and particularly describing the place to be searched, and the persons or things to be seized.

refer to "persons," not "citizens," so even many illegal immigrants have been found entitled to key constitutional protections. But U.S. constitutional rights do not protect every non-citizen physically in the U.S. Generally, the more formalized or lengthy the immigrant's stay in the U.S., the more rights he or she has.)

Eighteenth-century law and custom assumed generally that the most important man of a household governed its women, children, servants, and, where locally permitted, slaves. "Privacy" at that time included the notion that the state should not interfere with such men's authority over their private domains, even to prevent abuse.[2]

Privacy Applied to the Individual

During the slow advance toward equality, a new idea emerged that privacy rights belong to individual people, no matter who or where they are. An 1890 article by Samuel Warren and future Supreme Court Justice Louis Brandeis is often credited with introducing privacy as a legal theory. This new way of thinking brought together constitutional protections against government interference, the ancient right against physical trespass, and newer rights against intrusion by parties other than the government. Their article popularized one of the most enduring legal definitions of privacy, as "the right to be let alone." They wrote: "The intensity and complexity of life, attendant upon advancing civilization, have rendered necessary some retreat from the world, and man, under the refining influence of culture, has become more sensitive to publicity, so that solitude and privacy have become more essential to the individual; but modern enterprise and invention have, through invasions upon his privacy, subjected him to mental pain and distress, far greater than could be inflicted by mere bodily injury."[3]

In 1928, most of the U.S. Supreme Court still viewed the Fourth Amendment as literally protecting "persons, houses, papers and effects"—that is, private property, or private spaces such as a person's car or clothing—not private communication. In

Olmstead v. United States, the Court majority opinion said federal agents enforcing the anti-alcohol Prohibition laws did not need a warrant to tap phone lines used by a liquor smuggler named Olmstead. It said the agents who listened to Olmstead's calls could not have violated his Fourth Amendment rights because they did not physically enter his property. This provoked an angry dissenting opinion from Justice Brandeis, in which he spoke of the "right to be let alone" as "the most comprehensive of rights and the right most valued by civilized men."[4]

It was not until the 1967 case of *Katz v. United States* that the Court changed its doctrine, saying that "the Fourth Amendment protects people, not places." Reversing the *Olmstead* decision, it held that a man who placed illegal bets using a pay phone had a "reasonable expectation of privacy," so the Fourth Amendment required police to respect his privacy unless a magistrate issued a warrant allowing them to eavesdrop.[5]

> **Is it reasonable to expect privacy when using a cell phone?**

Thanks to the widespread use of the Internet, a further transition is now in progress from wiretapping laws designed for telephones to new laws that are adapting with varying success to online and other electronic communications.

———————●————————●————————●———————

New technology makes privacy more easily invaded, and the terrorist attacks of September of 2001 have brought up urgent conflicts between privacy and security. Privacy violations helped provoke the American Revolution, and they appear prominently in the U.S. Constitution's Bill of Rights, but the legal theory of a "right to privacy" is only about 100 years old. As law and culture have shifted to favor individual equality, "privacy" has come to signify, not the right to exclude outsiders from a hierarchically ruled household, but the rights of equal individuals to "be let alone."

Not Everyone Can Be Safely "Let Alone"

In a perfect world, perhaps people could be "let alone." In fact, though, responsible people do need to intrude on others' privacy for everyone's benefit.

Too much privacy can be as bad as too little. Without agreed rules, bullies and cheats would take over. Rules need enforcing, and enforcement requires invasions of privacy. Banning security cameras would make robberies easier. Banning Internet and telephone surveillance would assist fraud, terrorism, and other crime. Treating the household as off-limits to outsiders would condone domestic abuse. Banning health and safety inspections of businesses would disable consumer protection laws. Private authorities also have to engage in intrusive supervision. Parents have to protect children from their own mistakes. Employers have to guard against theft. Psychiatrists whose patients make threats have to pass on warnings.

14

In a crisis, it is reasonable to sacrifice some privacy to security.

Democratic countries are constantly negotiating the balance between personal privacy and public safety. With the attacks of September 11, 2001, that balance shifted in the United States to favor security over privacy more often. Congress and state legislatures passed new laws allowing increased investigation powers to police and federal agents.[1]

Advocates of such laws argued that showing too much respect for constitutional rights during a terrorism crisis would hurt public safety. The federal appeals judge Richard Posner argued in December of 2001 that civil libertarians wrongly "treat our existing civil liberties—freedom of the press, protections of

Items confiscated from passengers at the Baltimore-Washington airport in 2002. Almost any object can be used as a weapon in one way or another, but airport authorities try to remove those with the greatest potential to inflict injury. What some see as a necessity, others call a useless inconvenience—but many consider the inconvenience well worthwhile for the increased security it brings.

privacy and of the rights of criminal suspects, and the rest—as sacrosanct, insisting that the battle against international terrorism accommodate itself to them."

He wrote:

> I consider this a profoundly mistaken approach to the question of balancing liberty and security. The basic mistake is the prioritizing of liberty. It is a mistake about law and a mistake about history. . . . We are a nation under law, but first we are a nation. . . . The law is a human creation rather than a divine gift. . . . It is an instrument for promoting social welfare, and as the conditions essential to that welfare change, so must it change.[2]

That same month, Attorney General John Ashcroft told a Senate committee, "To those who scare peace-loving people with phantoms of lost liberty, my message is this: Your tactics only aid terrorists, for they erode our national unity and diminish our resolve."[3]

Crisis can drive governments to methods that otherwise might be called racist. In June of 2002, Jeff Jacoby of *The Boston Globe* argued the country should get over its "politically correct" scruples and use frankly race-based "profiling" as a guide for airport searches. He noted that former Vice Presidents Al Gore and Dan Quayle had both been searched at airports, and wrote, "Every minute spent patting down Al Gore or an elderly man in a wheelchair is a minute not spent focusing attention on a passenger who has a higher likelihood of actually being a hijacker. A passenger named Abdullah, say, who is 24 years old and a citizen of Saudi Arabia. . . ."[4]

What conclusions, if any, can be drawn from a person's ethnic background or style of dress?

What kind of information is it fair to use in deciding whom to suspect of intending harm?

Almost immediately after the attacks of September of 2001, the Department of Justice asked Congress for new powers based on two main arguments: the ancient principle that a government needs more authority in times of danger, and the subtler, more modern argument that the law needs to adapt to new technologies and criminal methods. In a speech he gave on September 17, 2001, Ashcroft was already calling for "comprehensive" new legislation affecting "criminal justice, immigration, intelligence gathering and financial infrastructure."[5]

Congress quickly enacted many of those proposals, principally through the Uniting and Strengthening America by Providing Appropriate Tools Required to Intercept and Obstruct Terrorism (USA PATRIOT) Act, which passed almost unanimously in October of 2001.

Among many provisions, PATRIOT permits investigators to obtain search warrants more easily and it lets judges authorize broader searches with a single warrant. This includes permission for "roving wiretaps" that allow investigators to tap any communication device used by a given person, not

America Under the USA PATRIOT Act: Not America?

... Of course, there is no doubt that if we lived in a police state, it would be easier to catch terrorists. If we lived in a country that allowed the police to search your home at any time for any reason; if we lived in a country that allowed the government to open your mail, eavesdrop on your phone conversations, or intercept your email communications; if we lived in a country that allowed the government to hold people in jail indefinitely based on what they write or think, or based on mere suspicion that they are up to no good, then the government would no doubt discover and arrest more terrorists.

But that probably would not be a country in which we would want to live. And that would not be a country for which we could, in good conscience, ask our young people to fight and die. In short, that would not be America....

—Senator Russ Feingold (D-Wisconsin),
explaining his vote against the USA PATRIOT Act

just a specific line or telephone. PATRIOT reduces barriers to eavesdropping on telephones, voice mail, and e-mail. It increases the use of secret "sneak and peek" searches, and makes it easier for investigators to get warrants for personal information kept by institutions, such as medical and library records. It creates new, broader definitions of terrorism and of helping terrorists.

One report in September of 2002 suggested the Department of Justice had had good reasons for wanting "roving wiretap" powers. The Associated Press quoted federal spokesmen as saying, "Government agents have recently uncovered numerous calls from difficult-to-track prepaid cell phones, Internet-based phone service, prepaid phone cards and public pay phones in the United States to known al-Qaida locations overseas. . . ."[6]

With the November 2002 passage of the Homeland Security Act, Congress further helped public officials to gather and compare records about people suspected of terrorism connections. The law consolidated many federal functions under a single Department of Homeland Security and allowed for more comprehensive analysis of information about members of the public in government and private databases. The newer law does not do as much as PATRIOT to increase surveillance powers directly, but it makes government investigation easier in some ways—in particular, it encourages private individuals and organizations to give information to the government voluntarily by protecting them from lawsuits if they do so. Critics have noted this could encourage Internet service providers to give their customers' e-mails to the government. The legislation also provides for the appointment of a Privacy Officer and an Officer for Civil Rights and Civil Liberties, and several other provisions address privacy rights. However, privacy advocates have criticized the laws as allowing too much government intrusion into private lives.[7]

Also in November of 2002, news emerged that the Defense Advanced Research Projects Agency had created an "Information Awareness Office" to manage a new, dramatically titled

"Total Information Awareness" system. This project was to work on techniques for finding possible terrorists by "mining" large compilations of data for suspicious patterns.[8]

As terrorism arrestees find their way to public trial, it will become easier to assess how much the new laws have done to protect the public. Certainly each time a plot is proven to have been thwarted through surveillance, the argument will be stronger that a democratic society's protectors do need to invade individual privacy to do their jobs.

Search and seizure law has to change constantly.

The current liberty-security debate is not about absolutes — it is neither a question of trampling all rights, nor of stopping all investigations. There is and was substantial agreement about many situations in which the government may invade personal privacy.

Americans have a "right to be let alone" by government officials, including police, unless a public officer has a good reason to think a particular person is breaking the law. However, the Fourth Amendment only protects personal privacy up to a point. An officer's duty to protect the public often outweighs a suspect's "right to be let alone."

Under the Fourth Amendment warrant requirement, a police officer who wants to conduct a search must present an acceptable level of proof to a magistrate. The magistrate does not have to be a judge, but must be "neutral and detached" and "capable of determining whether probable cause exists" for the search.[9]

> **What does it mean to "behave suspiciously"?**
>
> **Is this something that most people do at one time or another?**
>
> **How unusual does behavior have to be to become "suspicious"?**

In some cases a police officer may conduct a search or arrest without a warrant. The simplest of many examples is that a police officer who witnesses a crime may arrest the perpetrator. Within limits, officers may stop, pat-search, and question a person who is behaving suspiciously but not obviously breaking any law.[10]

Twentieth-century Supreme Court cases—notably *Weeks v. United States* and *Mapp v. Ohio*—created the "exclusionary rule," which requires that evidence obtained in violation of a suspect's Fourth Amendment rights must be excluded from that suspect's criminal trial.[11]

These are longstanding rules that are now being adjusted, not replaced, by new laws such as PATRIOT.

Serious security measures in public schools are necessary and effective.

The attacks of September of 2001 marked a turning point for antiterrorism efforts. A turning point for school security came earlier, with the Columbine High School massacre in Littleton, Colorado in the spring of 1999.

In August of 1999, as schools prepared for the first new academic year after Columbine, *The New York Times* reported, "[M]illions of students returning to class in the next few weeks will encounter a steely array of new security measures. In many schools, lockers are being removed, cameras are being installed as hallway monitors, and students will have to swipe a computerized ID card just to get in the door. . . ." Meanwhile, it said, some schools "have rejected the idea of detection systems, finding them an affront to educational openness, and are concentrating instead on a drumbeat of programs to make students feel more responsible for their school's safety and less reluctant to report violations."[12]

The *Times* quoted some administrators as saying school security measures have worked well and cited reports by the Department of Education and the Centers for Disease Control and Prevention showing gun-related problems in schools had decreased in the 1990s, which the article attributed to new school security efforts. CDC maintains a "Youth Risk Behavior Surveillance System" site[13] with statistics on

This school security tape was used as evidence in the 2001 trial of 14-year-old Nathaniel Brazill, charged with the murder of a teacher. More schools have installed security cameras in recent years to help stop violent crime on campus; the sacrifice of students' and administrators' personal privacy is seen as a necessity.

violence, tobacco use, and other dangers to teenagers' lives.

A report on school violence by the National Research Council said that although schools introduced new security procedures reluctantly, "in some circumstances, such measures are a welcome first step in restoring a sense of security," as in Chicago, where there were no more shootings after schools installed metal detectors. The report found that when schools hired police officers "they became a symbol and a rallying point for students and faculty who were concerned about security. They also served as a communication channel for students to report information about threats to school security. . . ."[14]

Even before Columbine, some school administrators had begun to take lockers out of hallways, arguing that lockers had become a discipline problem and a place to store drugs and weapons.[15]

Schools are finding they must count in part on students themselves to report threats or violent fantasies told to them by classmates. An *Education Week* article early in 2001 said most students who perpetrated shooting incidents had told others what they intended to do, directly or indirectly.[16]

The leading Supreme Court decision on minor students' privacy is the 1985 case of *New Jersey v. T.L.O.* An assistant principal, Theodore Choplick, searched the purse of a 14-year-old girl identified as T.L.O. who was accused of smoking cigarettes. He found marijuana and evidence that she was dealing the drug. She was "found to be a delinquent" in juvenile court. She appealed the case, saying the search of her purse violated her Fourth Amendment rights. The Supreme Court ruled that students do have Fourth Amendment rights against searches by public school officials, but they have fewer rights than adults in the outside world. It said Mr. Choplick did not need a warrant or even full probable cause for the search so long as it was reasonable given the circumstances and the amount of suspicion.[17]

> **Does it make sense that the Court approved of searching T.L.O.'s purse but protected her privacy by concealing her name on court papers?**

Violating privacy can save lives.

Professional ethics ordinarily require doctors, clergy, therapists, and lawyers to keep their clients' or patients' secrets, so that people can feel safe speaking freely to them. In many cases— though not all—such professionals are exempted from testifying in court about confidences. Professionals are divided, however, about what to do when a patient or client announces a serious intention to hurt someone.

In 1969, a student named Prosenjit Poddar told his therapist at a University of California hospital that he intended to kill a classmate who had rejected his romantic advances. The therapist was worried enough to call the campus police, and he tried to get Poddar hospitalized. However, he did not make the effort to identify and warn Poddar's intended victim.

Her name was Tatiana Tarasoff. Poddar murdered her in October of 1969. In a lawsuit brought by Tatiana's parents, the California Supreme Court decided Poddar's therapist should have "exercised reasonable care" by either warning the threatened victim or restraining his patient. The *Tarasoff* decision only affected California directly, but courts in many other states have endorsed it.[18]

Governments need to intervene in households to stop abuse and enforce family responsibilities.

The idea that an abused member of a household can turn to the outside world for help has always existed in some form, but it is only recently that government has intervened regularly to stop private bullying. Once it would have been considered tyrannical for a government to interfere with the authority of a husband over a wife, or of parents over children. Now our society recognizes that public and private tyrannies are equally bad, and a

FROM THE BENCH

From *Tarasoff v. Regents of the University of California,* 17 Cal.3d 425, 339–340 (Cal., 1976)

...Weighing the uncertain and conjectural character of the alleged damage done the patient by such a warning against the peril to the victim's life, we conclude that professional inaccuracy in predicting violence cannot negate the therapist's duty to protect the threatened victim.

The risk that unnecessary warnings may be given is a reasonable price to pay for the lives of possible victims that may be saved....

democratic government sometimes needs to protect less powerful individuals from mistreatment in the home.

At the same time, government has begun to act more vigorously in enforcing parents' responsibilities to children, especially fathers' duties to provide child support. Paul Legler, a federal child support enforcement official, wrote in 2000 that social attitudes have changed in favor of identifying fathers and enforcing their child support obligations. At the same time, hospital procedures have changed to press fathers to acknowledge paternity on the day of their children's birth, and DNA testing has made it possible to prove fatherhood in disputed cases. Legler wrote: "Establishing paternity was seen as a way to alleviate some poverty because doing so opened the door to the possible receipt of child support. A rising body of evidence showed that most unwed fathers could pay some support for their children. . . ."[19]

> **When is it time to act to stop someone else's angry behavior?**

The 1996 Personal Responsibility and Work Opportunity Reconciliation Act (PRWORA), best known as federal "welfare reform," called on states to set up genetic testing and paternity acknowledgment procedures, required mothers receiving welfare to help pursue fathers for child support, and ordered the creation of state "new-hires databases" to ensure that each new employee gets listed on a nationwide Federal Parent Locator Service. This measure does invade privacy, but at the same time it protects thousands of children from poverty.[20]

Employers need to supervise employees.

It would be nice if everyone had work that they liked and did well. Such is not the case. Supervisors have to counteract the effects of boredom, laziness, and dishonesty, to spot carelessness, and to guide inexperience.

Perhaps not every supervisor will count employees' computer keystrokes, watch work stations with security cameras, or record customer service calls "for quality purposes," but supervision does involve invasions of privacy.[21] For example, if an employee uses an office e-mail account to run a rival business on the side, the employer should be able to find out and take action. If a telephone order-taker is being chronically rude to customers, a supervisor may want to listen in. If friends are exchanging pornography on company computers in a way that harasses their coworkers, the employer actually has a legal obligation to intervene. Or suppose a forklift driver for a chemical company comes to work displaying the jerky movements and staccato speech of amphetamine abuse. The supervisor sees an accident waiting to happen. The driver claims to be ready for a day's work hoisting barrels of poisons. Shouldn't the employer be able to settle the question with a drug test?

As this last example suggests, the more an employee's mistakes might cause harm, the more intrusion tends to get approval. The Supreme Court issued two parallel decisions on workplace drug testing in 1989: *Skinner v. Railway Labor Executives' Assn.* and *Treasury Employees v. Von Raab*. *Skinner* allowed the federal government to require alcohol and drug testing for railroad employees involved in accidents or safety violations. *Von Raab* allowed the Customs Service to require drug tests from applicants for work involving drug enforcement, guns, or government secrets. These were relatively narrow permissions, allowing testing on special occasions only, but still they established the principle that it can be proper to test people who are not individually suspected of wrongdoing.[22]

Medical tests, such as drug tests and DNA sampling, are necessary to protect the public.

Since the *Skinner* and *Von Raab* decisions on employee testing, the Supreme Court has endorsed drug testing for high school athletes, and, as of 2002, for all participants in public schools' competitive extracurricular activities.

For high school students, random testing was first permitted in 1995, when *Vernonia School Dist. 47J v. Acton* allowed an

**DRUG-
FREE
SCHOOL
ZONE**

HIGH PROFILE
ENFORCEMENT AREA

VIOLATIONS IN THIS AREA
WILL BE AGGRESSIVELY
PROSECUTED

ATTORNEY GENERAL'S OFFICE
DEPARTMENT OF EDUCATION

Schools can be volatile places, and administrations tend to impose heavy restrictions on access and behavior. But, many argue, if the goal is to create an environment in which students can concentrate on learning and not worry about crime, then is it a good idea to fill that environment with fences and heavy-handed warnings?

Oregon school district to impose drug testing on all its high school athletes, after discovering that some athletes were at the center of an increasing school drug culture.[23]

Justice Scalia based his decision on *Skinner* and *Von Raab*, on the idea that athletes already give up some privacy by undressing in locker rooms, and the argument that student athletes are "children," so they have fewer legal rights than adults, and the adults supervising them—acting in the place of their parents—have a duty to protect them from drugs.

In June of 2002, the Supreme Court went even farther with *Board of Education of Independent School District No. 92 of*

Pottawatomie County v. Earls. This decision expanded the *Vernonia* decision about sports by endorsing a school policy in Tecumseh, Oklahoma that required all middle and high school students to agree to random drug testing before they could join extracurricular school activities.[24]

The Court's majority opinion confirmed under *T.L.O.* that high school students do have Fourth Amendment rights but still justified the tests, saying, "in the context of safety and administrative regulations, a search unsupported by probable cause may be reasonable 'when "special needs, beyond the normal need for law enforcement, make the warrant and probable-cause requirement impracticable."'"[25]

> **Does undressing in a locker room give up privacy in the same way as providing a urine sample for testing?**

DNA testing is even more personal than drug testing, yet it is now used routinely not just to determine the fathers of babies, but also to match suspects' genetic codes against crime scene evidence. In several cases DNA evidence has freed people who were serving long prison terms for crimes they did not commit.[26]

Especially in crisis times, responsible people have to invade others' privacy to protect public safety. Increases in government surveillance powers are necessary to meet new threats and technologies. These changes represent a difference only of degree: the Fourth Amendment has never offered more than partial protection for privacy. School security, including drug testing, has to be stricter in these troubled times. Government properly intervenes in households to protect against abuse, and supervisors properly step in to keep employees from causing harm to their employers or others. Even therapists sometimes have to break confidentiality to disclose threats, and drug and DNA testing can be necessary to protect the public welfare.

Too Much Official Invasion of Privacy Harms the Public Interest

Freedom and security are not opposites, and, as Benjamin Franklin once said, "They that can give up essential liberty to obtain a little temporary safety deserve neither liberty nor safety."[1]

True, some people cannot be trusted, but, as the Roman satirist Juvenal asked, "Who will guard the guards themselves?"[2] In practice, even undeserved trust is a wiser choice than excessive suspicion.

Privacy rights are especially important when a sense of crisis encourages scapegoating.

History exhibits extreme caution whenever anyone proposes to resolve a crisis by strengthening the police. Even in the United States, with its comparatively democratic tradition, nationally shared fear has at times led people to commit or tolerate violations of rights in the name of security.

In the 1790s, many Americans saw France as a dangerous place because of the series of bloody purges, known as the Reign of Terror, that followed the 1789 French Revolution. In 1798 Congress passed the Alien and Sedition Acts, which allowed the president to order immigrants out of the country at will and made it a crime to criticize the government. Writing a politically angry private letter was enough to get a person investigated.[3]

President Lincoln openly suspended the right of habeas corpus—the right not to be imprisoned without proper legal process—during the U.S. Civil War in the 1860s. During World War I, the Espionage Act punished peaceful anti-draft and anti-government speech as harshly as spying for the enemy. Also during World War I, volunteer members of the American Protective League, acting mainly—though not always—with official Justice Department approval, investigated people who seemed generally unpatriotic, draft-age men who were not in uniform, and people reported to the League by nervous citizens as possible spies or saboteurs.[4]

> **Is an American citizen safe from false accusation if he or she has nothing to hide?**

In 1919, a group of actual and attempted terrorist bombings led to a "Red Scare" that inflamed fears of the 1917 Russian Revolution spreading to the United States. The Palmer Raids, named after Attorney General A. Mitchell Palmer, arrested thousands of allegedly left-wing immigrants, mistreating many and deporting some to Russia.[5]

After the Japanese military attacked Pearl Harbor in December of 1941, federal officials feared people of Japanese descent would sabotage U.S. coastal defenses. Federal attention to Japanese Americans and European "enemy aliens" started with FBI searches of homes and quickly became more serious. In the spring of 1942 the government "evacuated" a few thousand Germans and Italians, and more than 110,000 Japanese

Americans, away from the West Coast. Most were imprisoned in "relocation camps" for most of the war. Evidence emerged in the 1980s that government attorneys who justified the Internment to the Supreme Court had concealed reports by several agencies, including the FBI, saying there was no evidence of danger to the country from Japanese Americans.[6]

The partly genuine danger of Soviet spying after World War II led to Senator Joseph P. McCarthy's famous hearings on the alleged U.S. influence of the Communist Party. The FBI, under its legendary mid-century chief, J. Edgar Hoover, conducted surveillance and investigations accompanying these hearings. This made the years from 1948 through the 1950s into a frightening time not only for the few actual Soviet spies, but also for thousands of Americans facing guilt by association because they had joined left-wing organizations, signed petitions, or helped Communist-identified causes such as Russian war relief.

In 1971, public reports began to emerge that the FBI had been operating what it called a "Counterintelligence Program," or "COINTELPRO" against American citizens since 1956. This program used military intelligence tactics to spy on political groups and disrupt members' lives. A parallel FBI effort spied on the non-violent civil rights leader Martin Luther King, Jr. and once sent him a tape of his own secretly recorded conversations with a letter apparently suggesting he commit suicide.[7]

Is it reasonable to watch immigrants more carefully than other people?

How long does an immigrant have to be in the United States before he or she is no longer perceived as an immigrant?

In the fall of 2001, after the September attacks and the October anthrax scare, security officials decided they could not be too careful. At airports, travelers had to stand in line for hours and give up their nail clippers as "contraband." After a terrorist tried to detonate a bomb in his shoe, some travelers were made

J. Edgar Hoover, shown here in 1934, directed the U.S. Bureau of Investigation (later known as the FBI), from 1924 until his death in 1972. His methods were legendary for their invasions of personal privacy.

to take off their shoes at security gates. The columnist Jon Carroll groused, "This will seem comforting right up until the first trouser bomb is discovered. That will make flying even more of a joy than it already is."[8]

Investigators began to question, search, and even imprison people, especially immigrants, based on guesses that they might know something about terrorism. The FBI questioned people who fit "profiles" but were not suspected of breaking any law.

Some 1,200 immigrants were detained for months on minor charges or none at all, and were in some cases deprived of basic rights such as medical treatment and attorney visits. Most of these initial detainees have now reportedly been cleared of suspicion and/or deported. The Justice Department is still refusing to release the names of some detainees and is asserting the authority to close immigration hearings to the public.[9]

In response to such events, people have begun to retell the old stories from 1798 to 1971 to recall that, in a crisis, the United States' democratic tradition has to be defended as resolutely as its physical borders.

The Department of Justice requested and got alarming new powers with the PATRIOT Act. It has also claimed the authority to make major policy changes under existing law.

The Homeland Security Act, by making it easier for the government to combine large amounts of private data from public and business sources, could have even more frightening results in the long run. Critics including Senator Bill Nelson (D-Florida) have expressed fears that the new Homeland Security Department's research division—and possibly also the Defense Department's new "Total Information Awareness" project— could end up gathering huge amounts of private material, such as e-mails and credit card records, without using warrants, on people who are not even suspected of any crime.

There was special concern in 2002 over the appointment of former Admiral John Poindexter to run the Information Awareness Office. In a prosecution linked to his role in the 1987 Iran-Contra scandal, Poindexter was convicted of five felonies that included destroying official documents and lying to Congress. He defeated the convictions on appeal only because they were based in part on testimony he had given under a promise of immunity from prosecution.[10]

Together these changes are removing safeguards that Congress and a concerned executive branch imposed on police powers in the 1960s and 1970s. These include lifting the Justice

Department's self-imposed 1976 ban on FBI undercover atten-
dance at political and religious meetings, and reducing the
Foreign Intelligence Surveillance Act's barriers between policing
citizens and spying on foreign enemies. This would be bad
enough if it were turning back the clock. It could possibly be
worse because the technological advances of the past 30 years
offer new surveillance possibilities to a government willing to
use them.[11]

Search and seizure law is slanted in favor of the police.

Criminal defense lawyers now comment on the Fourth Amendment with nostalgia rather than hope. There are now a tremen-
dous number of court-defined exceptions to the warrant rule that
let officers make searches or arrests without a magistrate's advance
permission. The warrant requirement is still officially the rule,
"reasonable" warrantless searches still officially the exception,
and "unreasonable" searches still unconstitutional, but courts
today endorse searches more easily than they did some years
ago. Discussing a 1991 case allowing the warrantless search of a
container in a car, Justice Scalia wrote: ". . . Even before today's
decision, the 'warrant requirement' had become so riddled with
exceptions that it was basically unrecognizable. In 1985, one
commentator cataloged nearly 20 such exceptions, including
'searches incident to arrest . . . automobile searches . . . border
searches . . . administrative searches of regulated businesses . . .
exigent circumstances . . . search[es]
incident to nonarrest when there is
probable cause to arrest . . . boat board-
ing for document checks . . . welfare
searches . . . inventory searches . . . airport searches . . . school search[es]. . . .'

> Do people who support more surveillance expect that they themselves will be watched more?

. . . Since then, we have added at least two more. *California v.
Carney* . . . (searches of mobile homes); [and] *O'Connor v. Ortega*
. . . (searches of offices of government employees). . . ."[12]

"Garbology," the bane of celebrities, has legitimate applications in law enforcement: here, FBI investigators collect evidence from garbage at the house of Oklahoma City bombing accomplice Terry Nichols. Many members of the modern consumer culture assume that a thing thrown away disappears forever—but this is not the case.

Justice Scalia went on to argue it was wrong to presume warrants were always required unless the circumstances fit a specifically defined exception. He argued that in many cases a court could find a warrantless search "reasonable" even though it did not fit a previously defined exception. However, the Court majority has not taken this step. Attorneys who take the criminal defense side want to preserve the warrant application process because it can stop unfair searches from happening in the first place, instead of just criticizing them after the fact.

High security in schools is making bad citizens — and bad backs.

Of course youth crime is a problem, but the security measures now in place at some high schools are problematic, too.

The same National Research Council discussion whose defense of security measures appears earlier in this book also said,

> An important question is whether and how mobilization to oppose violence in the schools ... might be aided by the installation of specialized security arrangements, including metal detectors, fences, identity badges, and the hiring of various kinds of security specialists.
>
> It is easy to understand the opposition to such measures. They can change the look and feel of the school from a learning community to an anxiety-ridden prison. They can draw attention to the fact that the social relations have so frayed that schools have to rely on technology and rules instead of human relationships and values to provide security. Such measures can distract students, faculty, and administrators from the important work of teaching, including teaching the idea of what it means to be a responsible school citizen. . . . [13]

While endorsing metal detectors and police officers, the report found it was useless to put fences around schools because outsiders were not the problem.

FROM THE BENCH

From *In re Adam,* 697 N.E. 2d 1100 (Ohio App.1997)

. . . [O]ne cannot envision any rule which minimizes the value of our Constitutional freedoms in the minds of our youth more dramatically than a statute which proclaims that juveniles have no right to privacy in their personal possessions. . . . It is hypocritical for a teacher to lecture on the grandeur of the United States Constitution in the morning and violate its basic tenets in the afternoon.

In the case of lockers, does it help anything to take away students' only private space at school? A Santa Monica physical therapist, Lori Rubenstein, has suggested there may be harmful physical effects on children and teenagers in schools without lockers who have to carry heavy bookbags: "Students who have lockers and get to use them between classes did not have the physical complaints of headaches, back pain and spinal numbness that those without lockers [did]."[14]

As for asking students to report signs of violence, Darcia Harris Bowman also said in her *Education Week* article that in several real cases, students could have stopped school attacks by calling authorities about a classmate's suspicious behavior, but they either did not take the danger signs seriously or did not want to tattle to adults. The article said students see adult authorities as opponents and are not easily persuaded that classmates they report will be helped rather than punished.[15] Routinely treating students as suspects will not build a school into a community likely to cooperate for everyone's sake if a genuine threat appears.

Troubled people need to be able to speak freely in confidence.

After the *Tarasoff* decision required California therapists to reveal threatening confidences, some patients with aggression problems stopped or avoided treatment or "could not use it effectively out of fear of being betrayed." Some members of the profession felt it changed psychotherapists' jobs by turning them into guardians of public safety and not just healers.[16]

> **Does a person who learns of a planned violent act have an obligation to warn others?**
>
> **If so, which others?**
>
> **How serious does the danger have to be?**

State bar organizations have taken a more reserved approach to lawyers' duties in cases where clients confess threatening intentions in confidence. Some states, including California, require attorneys to keep clients' confidences no matter what. Nevertheless, attorneys are taught in school, and generally agree privately, that if they know of a real physical threat to another person, the only moral action is to try to stop the harm while trying to minimize bad effects on the client.[17]

While professionals' breaches of confidence may prevent some violent incidents, it is also possible that people who could be counseled out of violent intentions will now choose not to seek help.

Invading the household sets a dangerous precedent.

History teaches that when countries abolish respect for household privacy, they are no longer safe places to live.

The totalitarians of Nazi Germany and Soviet Russia often talked publicly about the importance of the family, but in fact they could not stand the traditional idea of the home as a place of refuge from the outside world. They tried to extend their power everywhere.

The feminist scholar Kate Millett finds both regimes treated the family as a unit of government. The Nazis especially opposed abortion and contraception, and both regimes eventually

FROM THE BENCH

From *Brinegar v. United States*, 338 U.S. 160 (1949) (Jackson, J., dissenting)

...Uncontrolled search and seizure is one of the first and most effective weapons in the arsenal of every arbitrary government. And one need only briefly to have dwelt and worked among a people possessed of many admirable qualities but deprived of these rights to know that the human personality deteriorates and dignity and self-reliance disappear where homes, persons and possessions are subject at any hour to unheralded search and seizure by the police....

banned abortion. Both treated parents as representatives of the government assigned to raise children according to required principles.[18]

In the United States, perhaps the most resented kind of government interference in the family is when social workers decide too quickly that a child needs protection. A California court recently found a social worker violated a mother's Fourth Amendment rights by taking away her children without a warrant in a situation with no physical danger: the social worker had thought the children might suffer emotional abuse. In another case, hospital staff repeatedly accused a Tennessee couple of abusing their baby, when in fact he was ill with rare diseases that caused weight loss and bleeding. Eventually a court found no abuse had occurred.[19]

One very old controversy concerns whether poor people must give up privacy in return for government assistance. This controversy has surrounded the federal welfare program since its creation in 1935. Some of the worst prying happened in the 1950s, when welfare workers would raid a household late at night to determine whether a single mother receiving benefits was living with a man. If so, they would label him a "substitute father," claim he was responsible for supporting the children, and cut the family off public aid.[20]

Do people give up some privacy rights by accepting government benefits?

What kinds of government benefits?

After a period of greater respect for welfare mothers' freedoms in the 1970s, the trend over the past twenty years has been toward welfare laws aimed at changing behavior. One of these is the 1996 PRWORA requirement that all mothers receiving TANF or Food Stamps must "cooperate" in state efforts to collect child support payments. A 1997 study suggested women often refused to point out their children's fathers to the government because they wanted the fathers to contribute informally when they could. But a report the following year found more serious reasons: some women expected their children's fathers would take violent revenge if they "cooperated."[21]

Employers should not interfere in employees' personal lives.

At one time there was not much legal distinction between business employees and household servants. But as the modern workplace evolved, employers and employees began to contract "at arm's length," in business relationships under rules different from those of a private household. For a while some employers tried to combine paternalism—a father's too-personal, though possibly well-meaning, authority—with large-scale production, but the two ideas were incompatible.

In the 1880s the Pullman Company, maker and operator of rail passenger cars, built a tidy, wholesome, but oppressive "company town" for its workers and their families. The town offered its own school, church, athletic programs, band, theater, and library. Rents, however, were high, and dissent not tolerated. The company fired factory workers who ran for office against Pullman candidates. Liquor was banned and informing encouraged. Residents of the Pullman town resented these methods, especially when the company imposed pay cuts. In 1894 the Pullman Company suffered one of the most dramatic strikes in U.S. history.[22]

Employers still do try to direct their employees' lives, though perhaps not so heavy-handedly. In workplaces, as in other contexts, supervision can take the form of panopticism—an idea that dates back at least to the 18th-century English philosopher and inventor Jeremy Bentham. Bentham's panopticon design is still used in prisons—and sometimes even in shopping malls. It consists of a circular building lined with cells on its inner walls, all watched from a central guard tower. The philosopher Michel Foucault commented, "All that is needed . . .

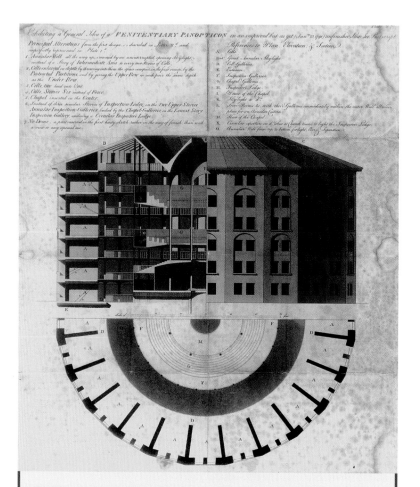

Bentham's Panopticon aimed to give authorities complete control over prisoners through a disparity in access to information: the guards would be able to see the prisoners at all times, but the prisoners never would see the guards. A circular design would enable guards to survey cells easily from a central tower, thick walls would isolate the prisoners from one another, and blinds and specially constructed chambers in the central tower would ensure that no prisoner ever knew exactly when a guard was watching. The idea of panopticism has been picked up recently as a model of the information age and is important to understanding issues of modern privacy.

is to place a supervisor in a central tower and to shut up in each cell a madman, a patient, a condemned man, a worker or a schoolboy. . . ." Writers including Foucault and the urban critic Mike Davis have argued there is too much panopticism in modern life: sometimes in the form of literal surveillance, as with security cameras, and sometimes as one-way information gathering, like research by credit rating companies.[23]

Barbara Ehrenreich's first-person report on low-wage work, *Nickel and Dimed: On (Not) Getting By in America*, tells how employers convey a panopticon mentality through "personality tests." On Wal-Mart's version:

> . . . there are the usual questions about whether a coworker observed stealing should be forgiven or denounced, whether management is to blame if things go wrong, and if it's all right to be late when you have a 'good excuse.' . . . The real function of these tests, I decide, is to convey information not to the employer but to the potential employee, and the information being conveyed is always: You will have no secrets from us. We don't just want your muscles and that portion of your brain that is directly connected to them, we want your innermost self.[24]

Ehrenreich quotes a news report that as of 1999 employer personality testing "now supports a $400-million-a-year industry."

What can a multiple-choice personality test really say about a person?

Physical tests such as drug and DNA tests are almost never justified.

Every drug or DNA test carries the risk of mistakes or illicit snooping. Drug tests, if properly administered, are fairly accurate, and DNA tests extremely so. However, samples can get switched, and a sample given for one purpose can be used for another—for example, someone could run a pregnancy

A vice president of the LifeCodes Corporation in Connecticut shows probes used to test DNA patterns. DNA testing is now used to settle paternity disputes and to match suspects' genetic codes with samples collected at crime scenes; because DNA is the code of individual life itself, many worry that its applications will further endanger the very notion of privacy.

test on a urine sample given for drug testing, though it would probably be illegal to do so.

As DNA technology improves, the same stored samples of genetic material are likely to tell more about people as time goes on. Suppose a man gives a DNA sample to settle a paternity dispute. Suppose further that, regardless of whether it names him as the father, the lab report says he has a high risk for diabetes. He loses his insurance. Such a scenario is still imaginary, but soon it may not be.[25]

On drug tests, Ehrenreich quotes an ACLU report from 1999 as saying tests do not make employees more punctual or productive. She notes testing is expensive, especially if the cost of all the tests is divided by the number of drug users caught. She quotes 1990 figures of $11.7 million spent on 29,000 drug tests of federal employees, with 153 positive results. (It might, of course, be argued to the contrary that drug tests work, not by catching users, but by scaring people out of using drugs.)[26]

There might be a case for testing people who do physically dangerous work, like railroad employees, but when it comes to testing Wal-Mart stock clerks or news reporters at *The Miami Herald,* the humiliation and intrusion of urine sampling does not justify whatever vague dangers the tests might prevent.

After the 2002 *Pottawatomie* decision on school drug testing, critics said it seemed pointless to single out students for drug testing because they decided to take part in just the kinds of after-school activities that tend to discourage drug use.

> **Does drug testing reduce drug use?**

Lindsay Earls, whose high school experience was litigated in the Pottawatomie case, said, "I'm really sad that every other schoolkid in America might have to go through a humiliating urine test like I did just to join the choir or the debate team."[27]

———•———•———•———

History teaches that authorities often overreact to crisis in harmful ways. New dangers do not necessarily justify giving investigators new powers to invade privacy. In schools, workplaces, welfare offices, and police investigations, public and private enforcers already have too much power, and they can easily abuse it.

Civilized Life Requires the Exchange of Information

M odern life, especially urban life, requires giving up some privacy. People have to share private details with individuals and companies they know only by reputation, if at all. This is nothing new. Even in the pre-industrial world, people routinely agreed to trust messengers, locksmiths, doctors, and others who could exploit clients' secrets if they chose.

People who fulminate about the dangers of surveillance are most likely flattering themselves if they think marketing companies or the FBI have more than a generic interest in their doings. Real information technology is never quite as all-seeing as science-fiction imaginations would have us think. Likewise, it is technophobic to see electronic privacy risks as any more than a new twist on the ancient problem of trust.

Complex societies need the large data collecting and sorting systems that worry privacy advocates. Doctors, schools, employers, immigration and tax officials, building inspectors, and consumer regulators could not do their jobs without keeping files. Such files are increasingly computerized, but computerizing a record does not automatically make it less private. Public laws and private agreements can protect such information.

Do you know how many people have read your health records?

Do you know where your health records are kept?

It can also be important to reveal data about people against their wishes, for their own safety, the public's safety, or the safety of investments. People who bounce checks may find themselves on a list shared among banks that makes it more difficult for them to do the same thing again. Credit report agencies check with local courthouses for the names of tenants sued in eviction lawsuits. An insurance company paying for a hospital operation has a right to know what the doctor did and why.[1]

Reduced privacy is a fair price to pay for new services and amenities.

Thanks to advances in technology we can send e-mail halfway around the world in seconds, place telephone calls from almost any spot in the world, and download huge libraries of text, images, and sound. That is worth some loss of privacy.

At one time there was good reason to see consumer electronics as turning industrialized societies into glum collections of lonely people staring at television sets. Now an American staring at a screen, far from being isolated, may be swapping concert reviews with a music fan in Norway or inviting friends to a party. Easy mobile communications are creating new social phenomena, such as the "swarm," an instant crowd created by quick networking among cell phones and two-way pagers. The "swarm" has had silly applications, as among female admirers of Great Britain's Prince William who "swarm" wherever he appears in public. It has also had activist uses, as when former Philippine president Joseph Estrada became the subject of instantly organized demonstrations wherever he went.[2]

Although it is illegal to record cell phone calls without a warrant, cell phone conversations are not really private, even when the conversation is a confidential attorney-client conversation.[3]

Cell phones also broadcast the user's location as a side effect of being used, but some people see this function as a safety feature, not a drawback. Cell phone and pager signals were used to find victims after the attacks of September of 2001.

A group of high school students in Union City, California recently persuaded their state legislature to drop a ban on cell phones in school. The legislators had hoped the ban would discourage drug dealing. But the students said they wanted to be able to call the police or their parents in case of emergency. Four other states have already given up school cell phone prohibitions for safety reasons.

There is a similar privacy/service tradeoff in allowing oneself to be "profiled" through bank, credit card, or grocery discount card records, or in accepting "cookies" on the Internet. Cookies can store data on an Internet user's own computer to make websites appear to "remember" the user's interests. Some marketing database companies cooperate with commercial websites to gather a combined picture of browsers' interests that they can in turn use to target advertisements. For example, the DoubleClick company affiliates with several of the online news sources cited in this book. A person using this book to research privacy issues with a computer set to accept cookies would allow DoubleClick to gather a combined picture of the articles selected and therefore of the reader's research interests.

> **How much personal information would you exchange for a free web-based e-mail account? For a free cell phone? A car loan? A job with the government?**

But cookies are useful, too. They can store records of a customer's interests in books or music and recommend new books or recordings that the customer might have missed. Cookies allow users to personalize news and research sites for quick access to their favorite subjects.

Internet security measures such as e-mail encryption, anonymous browsing services, and secure servers are now available to users, sometimes assisted by cookies. Companies concerned for their image are careful to offer assurances about protecting customers' information. As consumers become better informed on these issues, companies will naturally have to provide privacy guarantees or risk losing their customers.[4]

Customer profiles developed through credit card purchase records can provide protection as well as convenience. This writer once celebrated a new job with a big trip to the mall, charging purchases of formal office wear and, on impulse, a pair of cowboy boots. The credit card company called that evening: had the card been stolen? It was a little unsettling to wonder why—was it the amount spent, or did the Western wear stand out from a customer profile marked "frumpy urban Yankee"? Still, it was nice to feel protected from fraud.

"Data mining"—the art of combining and searching data from many sources—can be a beneficial tool. Investigative reporters looking for public corruption have experimented since at least the 1980s with ways to filter databases for unusual clumps of information. Hospitals and medical plans

Personally Identifiable Information

Personally Identifiable Information is a phrase often used to define the duties of government agencies—and sometimes also businesses—to keep individual records private. In places like hospitals and welfare offices, this term may be used to distinguish between specific information that might hurt or embarrass a particular person if disclosed, and aggregated statistical information that can be used by researchers and planners and released to the public.

Definitions of *Personally Identifiable Information* vary. One of the simplest and narrowest is in the Video Privacy Protection Act [18 U.S.C. 2710(a)(3)]: "includes information which identifies a person as having requested or obtained specific video materials or services from a video tape service provider."

can now "mine" their patient records to find people whose risk factors suggest they ought to be screened for a serious disease, or to look for the causes of problems like infections acquired in hospitals.[5]

Data mining is also becoming an investigative tool for preventing terrorism—a use that is more controversial because it can involve filtering through the life details of innocent people in search of suspicious travel, spending, or communications.

Privacy protection methods are keeping up with technological changes.

Large institutions such as hospitals now take the management of confidential information very seriously. Medical information science is a topic for university doctoral degrees. Laws and regulations are beginning to build protections in this field in response to public concern.

One of Congress' major actions on health care data is the Health Insurance Portability and Accountability Act of 1996 (HIPAA), Public Law 104–191. This law in part authorizes an effort to store all U.S. health care information in a standardized, electronically movable format, so hospitals can share information easily to help patients in emergencies. At the same time, HIPAA creates new privacy protections to compensate for the fact that electronic record sharing makes it logistically easier to invade privacy.

Do you write to your doctor by e-mail?

If you don't, then why not?

Medical privacy is likely to be a political battleground for many years to come. But that is only to be expected. These are growing pains. Society will adjust to the new data technology, just as it adjusted to the invention of the telephone.

One scholar has suggested interestingly that it would help privacy to make the process for releasing medical records more awkward than it technologically has to be. He suggests people requesting records should have to submit paper release forms by hand, and hospital records clerks should be able to call up records only one at a time, not in large batches.[6]

Another suggestion for protecting privacy rights in material such as medical records is to give all individuals copyright-like ownership power to control what happens to information about them. This is impractical for free speech reasons, and because of the risk that if the laws turn an inalienable right into something that can be sold, then some people will actually sell it, even to their own disadvantage. Still, the idea is interesting food for thought.[7]

Congress and federal agencies can act effectively to protect privacy in specific areas, and they have done so.
After the actress Rebecca Schaeffer was stalked and murdered by an obsessed fan who got her driver's license information, Congress passed the Driver's Privacy Protection Act of 1994. The law prohibits motor vehicle departments from releasing personal information out of driver's license files except for a few specified reasons such as "matters of motor vehicle or driver safety and theft" and car manufacturers' product recalls. This law is still disputed, but it gives ordinary people's private information more protection than was once available, and the Supreme Court upheld it in 2000.[8]

Why Congress Acted to Protect DMV Records

. . . You may have gone to the trouble of getting an unlisted phone number and address, but the DMV will sell it anyway, to anyone who asks. That's what happened in California to Rebecca Schaeffer, promising young star of the television show 'My Sister Sam.' Although she had an unlisted home number and address, Ms. Schaeffer was shot to death by an obsessed fan who obtained her name and address through the DMV. In Iowa, a gang of thieves copied down the license plate numbers of expensive cars they saw, found out the names and addresses of the owners and robbed their homes at night. In Virginia, a woman regularly wrote to the DMV, provided the license plate numbers of drivers and asked for the names and addresses of the owners who she claimed were stealing the fillings from her teeth at night. . . .

—Rep. Jim Moran (D-Virginia) proposing the Driver's Privacy Protection Act

Similarly, after a news article based on video rental information helped defeat Judge Robert Bork's nomination to the Supreme Court, Congress passed the Video Privacy Protection Act, which forbids video stores in most cases from telling anyone other than the police what tapes a customer rents, and requiring that even the police must have a warrant, grand jury subpoena, or court order.[9]

Another effort to preserve consumers' privacy, this time for financial information from sources like bank accounts and credit cards, was the Gramm-Leach-Bliley Act, passed in 1999 as part of Public Law 106–102. It bans some sharing of information and devious practices such as "pretexting"—collecting information from consumers under false pretenses. There have been state efforts to impose tighter rules along these lines, including a consumer privacy measure that failed at the end of California's 2002 legislative session.[10]

Many personal disclosures are voluntary.

Encouraged by television, thousands of people have opened up private corners of their lives voluntarily—for money, to win a prize, or just for the excitement of being noticed.

Even 24-hour surveillance can be turned into entertainment. In George Orwell's *1984*, the phrase "Big Brother Is Watching You" described frightening surveillance by secret police. The "Big Brother" game show and most other "reality TV" programs involve people who volunteer to have millions of people watch them figure out how to live under challenging conditions. For many people, the prospect of fame overrides the emotional need for privacy. At ball games, when a roving camera magnifies the faces of fans in the stands, they tend to be flattered by the attention, not upset at the intrusion. People facing sad or grotesque family problems volunteer to be interviewed on talk shows although they risk being laughed at. The Internet is full of childhood memories, family vacation

How much would someone have to pay you to put your own diary on the Internet?

Or do you already have an online diary?

photos, disclosures of political opinion, personal diaries, and detailed conversations about the treatment of diseases that were once mentioned only in whispers.

A woman named Elizabeth gave birth to a son on the Internet in 1998. In 1999, another woman underwent breast cancer surgery online in order to encourage discussion about the disease. Jennifer Ringley has for five years charged subscribers to watch uncensored Web camera views of whatever she happens to be doing in her house. She writes, "I keep JenniCam alive not because I want to be watched, but because I simply don't mind being watched. . . ."[11]

Have you ever read the privacy policy of a website or computer application all the way through?

Do these sites assume that you will?

What if the policy contains something that you don't agree with?

Have you clicked "I accept" without knowing what you were accepting?

At a certain point, everyone has to decide what to disclose, for what price, if any. While prudent privacy measures are a good idea, it's difficult to live in the modern world while bracing oneself against every possibility of disclosure. Instead of a paranoid "trust nobody" approach, it may be healthier to take the view that old and new kinds of information gathering are not necessarily dangerous so long as society maintains control over them.

The need to trust strangers is as old as urban life itself. Information gathering is necessary to a complex modern society. Some laws have succeeded in limiting what public and private institutions do with information, and although most of us are in official databases whether we like it or not, a lot of the ways private companies gather information have to do with our own willingness to swap privacy for convenience or for small rewards like grocery discounts. The warnings we hear about the dangers of data gathering are probably overblown.

Institutions and Businesses Exploit Personal Information Unfairly

Scott McNealy, head of the computer company Sun Microsystems, famously commented in 1999, "You already have zero privacy. Get over it." McNealy has been quoted so often that it appears he touched a nerve.[1]

Should you get a small payment every time your name is transmitted electronically?

There is still such a thing as privacy, but once information (accurate or otherwise) gets into a list, it travels much farther than it used to. Disclosures that have been commonplace for decades, like handing over a credit card number, now involve new kinds of privacy risks.

Barriers to gathering and correlating information are dropping, to the point where researchers can reassemble much of the data trail that almost anyone creates through daily living.

Large-scale surveillance using cheap mechanical methods instead of live watchers is becoming easier, as technologies like voice and face recognition allow machines to do more of the watching. Some reports even suggest it is becoming possible for machines to do a crude form of mind-reading by capturing brain reactions to material such as photographs.[2] Website and credit card "privacy policies" that seem reassuring may have fine print retaining the ability to resell data. A given transaction can now find its way into any number of public and private "profiles."

"Data mining" makes it possible (though not necessarily legal) for a single researcher to combine material such as grocery bills, catalog orders, medical records, credit ratings, and online chat to produce a picture of a subject's taste in music, politics, and boyfriends; physical and mental health; and possibly, degree of resemblance to a criminal profile.[3] Now the PATRIOT and

FROM THE BENCH

From *Dwyer v. American Express Co.*, 652 N.E. 2d 1351, 1353 (Ill. App. 1 Dist. 1995)

Paraphrasing news descriptions of the American Express Company's "customer profile" practices, which were found not to violate Illinois law at the time:

... [D]efendants categorize and rank their cardholders into six tiers based on spending habits and then rent this information to participating merchants ... defendants analyze where they shop and how much they spend, and also consider behavioral characteristics and spending histories ... Defendants also offer to create lists which target cardholders who purchase specific types of items, such as fine jewelry. The merchants using the defendants' service can also target shoppers in categories such as mail-order apparel buyers, home-improvement shoppers, electronics shoppers, luxury lodgers, card members with children, skiers, frequent business travelers, resort users, Asian/European travelers, luxury European car owners, or recent movers....

Homeland Security laws make it more likely such activity will be treated as legal.

In early 2003 a federal district court ordered an Internet service provider to give information about a user to the Recording Industry Association of America, which claimed the user had illegally downloaded copyrighted music. This ruling enabled music companies to obtain by automatic subpoena— without having to obtain a court order—the names of users suspecting of receiving illegal downloads. As of this writing, this important decision was likely to be appealed.

Credit rating companies have significant control over Americans' lives, and a mistake on a credit report can cause serious problems. Under the federal Fair Credit Reporting Act, credit agencies are required to give out free copies of credit reports in specified circumstances, including to people denied credit, insurance, or employment because of reported bad credit. The agencies are required to investigate complaints and correct errors promptly; but in 2000 the three major companies paid a settlement of $2.5 million after the Federal Trade Commission established that they had been blocking consumers' inquiries.

As with many kinds of "permanent record" information, credit rating services hurt the old American idea of second chances. They may help landlords, employers, and mortgage bankers to avoid risk, but they also make it difficult for people who have made mistakes to move on with their lives.[4]

How important is it to keep strangers from knowing what you read on the Internet, if you don't read anything out of the ordinary?

What do you consider ordinary?

Consumers give up personal information too easily.

Fans of the Internet's JenniCam have to pay money to watch a woman who says she doesn't mind being watched, yet advertising companies manage to watch people for free without their consent.

In 2000, privacy advocates called on the Federal Trade Commission (FTC) to intervene after DoubleClick, Inc., bought the Abacus direct marketing company and proposed to combine the companies' databases. DoubleClick's main business is to put advertisements on websites. It tailors the ads to users' tastes, which it studies by using cookies to collect information about how users browse the Web. Abacus entered the merger with a huge archive of mailing lists containing U.S. residents' actual names and addresses.[5]

What upset the consumer advocates—and several state attorneys general—was that DoubleClick proposed to combine its "cookie" information with the name and address information from Abacus, resulting in detailed dossiers about Web users under their real names. After several lawsuits and an FTC investigation, DoubleClick backed off from its plan to merge the databases and settled the disputes, though some privacy advocates remained dissatisfied.[6]

Perhaps more alarming than cookies are "adware" and "spyware" programs. These programs, which often display banner advertisements, are available for download without cash payment. Users may not realize they are paying for the software in information: along with the advertised application, the program installs code that sends the user's personal "registration" information—name, address, phone number, and other details—to a series of advertisers. Such programs are not only intrusive, they can be difficult to remove. One company reportedly even used "spyware" to set up a distributed computing network that parasitically borrowed parts of users' computers to perform processing tasks for its advertising projects.[7]

Accidental disclosures are possible even from systems that make confidentiality a selling point. In 2002, Microsoft agreed to make changes in its Passport service after the Federal Trade Commission alleged that it provided less security than promised for materials such as credit card numbers and that its "Kids

Passport" system did not give parents full control over what information their children disclosed online.[8]

There are not enough new rules in place to protect old rights.

It is now technologically easy to combine data in one place that was collected for many different public and private purposes. This situation intensifies the need for barriers among types and sources of records.

Public uses of private data are a particular area for concern. The Federal Parent Locator Service, which identifies newly hired employees in order to enforce child support liability, is an example of this. Though the system may have been created with the best of intentions, it brings the United States slightly closer to the oppressive practice of registering and tracking all residents. Worse, it appeared in late 2002 that the new Homeland Security Department and the Defense Department's "Total Information Awareness" program would involve government investigative use of data gathered by private companies that are not subject to open-government laws or required to serve public-spirited purposes.

One of the major concerns about the USA PATRIOT Act is that it allows investigators to demand records, including business and library records, that were not created with law enforcement in mind. Librarians are not allowed to disclose requests for circulation information under PATRIOT's already notorious Section 215. However, *The Nation* reported that in an anonymous 2002 survey of 1,503 libraries, 85 said that "authorities (for example, FBI or police) requested information about their patrons pursuant to the events of Sept. 11." In the fall of 2001, a Pakistani-born scientist who bought technical manuals through the eBay online auction service was questioned about them by the FBI.[9]

Is there a moral difference between a police request for help solving a particular crime and a standing invitation to report anything suspicious?

In the summer of 2002, the Justice Department's "Operation TIPS" proposal provoked criticisms based on totalitarian history. As first proposed, TIPS would have recruited antiterrorism informers among public service workers, like mail carriers, whose jobs involved visiting private homes. By mid-August, combined liberal and conservative outrage had the Justice Department promising to scale back the program. In November of 2002, Congress' Homeland Security legislation banned TIPS entirely.[10]

The American Library Association (ALA) on Privacy in the Library

... Libraries are one of the great bulwarks of democracy. They are living embodiments of the First Amendment because their collections include voices of dissent as well [as] assent. Libraries are impartial resources providing information on all points of view, available to all persons regardless of age, race, religion, national origin, social or political views, economic status, or any other characteristic. The role of libraries as such a resource must not be compromised by an erosion of the privacy rights of library users.

The American Library Association regularly receives reports of visits by agents of federal, state, and local law enforcement agencies to libraries, where it is alleged they have asked for personally identifiable information about library users. These visits ... reflect an insensitivity to the legal and ethical bases for confidentiality, and the role it plays in the preservation of First Amendment rights, rights also extended to foreign nationals while in the United States. The government's interest in library use reflects a dangerous and fallacious equation of what a person reads with what that person believes or how that person is likely to behave. Such a presumption can and does threaten the freedom of access to information. It also is a threat to a crucial aspect of First Amendment rights: that freedom of speech and of the press include the freedom to hold, disseminate and receive unpopular, minority, "extreme," or even "dangerous" ideas. ...

—ALA, "Policy Concerning Confidentiality of Personally
Identifiable Information about Library Users"
www.ala.org/alaorg/oif/pol_user.html

Michele Kayal, an American editor, reacted to the original version of TIPS with an unhappy memory of life in Czechoslovakia (now the Czech Republic). She wrote that her landlady in Prague evicted her because neighbors informed on her, saying, for example, that she took showers too often, didn't make her bed, and "had a cat" (she had kept a friend's cat for a weekend). Kayal blamed this culture of informing on the years of Communist rule in Czechoslovakia, when people were expected to denounce each other's political or personal irregularities. She wrote that officially sponsored informing "erodes the soul of the watcher and the watched, replacing healthy national pride with mute suspicion, breeding insular individuals more concerned with self-preservation than with society at large. Ultimately it creates a climate that is inherently antithetical to security."[11]

The philosopher Hannah Arendt argued in the 1950s that "atomization"—turning society into a collection of lonely individuals, not a network of people who trust each other—was a key goal of both Nazi and Stalinist totalitarianism. In both societies, anyone, even a family member, might report to the government on anyone else.[12]

List-making should always be viewed with suspicion because it has been used for many purposes, including the worst. The Nazis' bigotry in the 1930s and 1940s went hand in hand with an energetic interest in classifying, labeling, and numbering their population. In each country where they took control, they conducted a census to categorize residents by religion and ethnicity. They later used these records to round up victims for the death camps.

The Japanese American Internment in the United States was not the same story. Internees in the United States had a wartime experience that, though unpleasant, was livable, a vast difference from the genocide in Europe. Still, the Internment did involve ethnic classifications and roundups within the United States on a larger scale than would be tolerated today. Although the Bureau of the Census refused to cooperate wholesale with the War Department in naming residents of Japanese descent, "it did provide small-area tabulations identifying concentrations of Japanese that clearly facilitated the internment effort. The bureau is decidedly uneasy about its role in this affair, for which it has been roundly criticized."[13]

These examples suggest it is worth thinking twice before creating any large database. Even information gathered with the best intentions and the firmest confidentiality promises may later be abused.

Sensitivity to the possible abuse of data affected the 2000 U.S. Census. In 2002 a census official wrote, ". . . [N]o matter how careful and devoted the Census Bureau is to protecting the confidentiality of personal information . . . , many people do not believe that their information will really be kept confidential."[14] Some members of Congress warned that people who avoided the census for confidentiality reasons were hurting their neighborhoods, because in many ways social service funds and voting power are distributed on the basis of census results. Rep. Rubén Hinojosa (D-Texas) compared ducking the census to "driving down the road and throwing $100 bills out the window."[15]

Since September of 2001, there has been debate about whether to create a nationwide identity card. Some say there is little difference between the state IDs and driver's licenses most people now carry and a federal ID. Others suggest a national identity card would be one more step toward centralized population registration, which the United States has avoided to date.

The laws Congress has passed to protect the most sensitive kinds of data—especially health information—provide some reassurance, but only patchy protection against the nuisance and intrusion of health-related advertising. A 2002 regulation interpreting HIPAA offered some privacy protections. It prohibited disclosing health information to employers without the patient's consent, and confirmed that patients may review their records and ask to have any mistakes changed. It also banned drug companies from directly buying patient information for advertising purposes. However, it continued to let the companies distribute "educational" publicity to specific people based on their health information—which is really a subtler form of advertising.[16]

Under federal law, students and their parents have a right to see their school records, and the records must be kept private in specified ways under the Family Education Records and Privacy Act (FERPA). However, FERPA privacy rights have many exceptions, including for releasing records to law enforcement. Schools may release or even sell "directory" information—name, address, telephone number, date and place of birth, field of study, awards, and type of diploma—providing they give each student or student's parents a chance to object.

Students and parents who disagree with material in school records, or feel the records violate their privacy, may challenge the material in a hearing, and may place their side of the story on file. The law protects students against having to answer surveys about their political opinions, sexual activity, parents'

Public Service or Marketing?

The Department clarifies that a communication that merely promotes health in a general manner and does not promote a specific product or service from a particular provider does not meet the general definition of 'marketing.' . . . [C]ommunications, such as mailings reminding women to get an annual mammogram, and mailings providing information about how to lower cholesterol, about new developments in health care (e.g., new diagnostic tools), about health or 'wellness' classes, about support groups, and about health fairs are permitted, and are not considered marketing.

—Department of Health and Human Services,
"Standards for Privacy of Individually Identifiable Health
Information, Final Rule," 67 FR 53182, 53189, August 14, 2002

incomes, and other sensitive subjects. Students who feel their FERPA rights have been violated can file a complaint asking the Secretary of Education to investigate. Note that FERPA gives most information and privacy rights to parents until students turn 18. It does not necessarily apply to immigrant or exchange students, nor can individuals invoke it in federal civil rights lawsuits.[17]

There are, of course, ways to live more privately—for example, using cell phones and credit cards sparingly, avoiding grocery discount cards, using browser settings and software to limit "cookies," and encrypting e-mail. But this is hardly a comprehensive list of precautions—there's probably no such thing, as the technology changes constantly—and it can be more trouble than it's worth to follow enough privacy precautions to avoid giving away free data. The better approach may be to ensure laws are passed that protect everyone from being invited, pressured, or forced to make so many kinds of disclosures.

Which ask for your ID more often: public officials or private businesses?

———•————•————•———

Privacy is in danger from private businesses that exploit data for marketing purposes, and from information sharing between public and private institutions. Overzealous investigators' use of privately compiled data is of special concern, as is the danger that official lists made for one purpose will be used for another. There are too many possible exceptions to laws that supposedly protect records from disclosure in areas such as health and education.

A Free Society Depends on the Right to Learn and Share Information

If privacy is no longer attainable, then at least it is possible to work toward transparency.

In his book *The Transparent Society*, the science fiction novelist David Brin argues that our privacy is basically gone, but we can still insist on "transparency": if large institutions can watch members of the public, the public should be able to watch them in return. For example, if police departments use cameras to watch city streets, there should also be Internet cameras in police stations so the public can check if officers are respecting suspects' rights.

> **What would "transparency" mean at the institutions you know best?**

Citing the proverb "People who live in glass houses shouldn't throw stones," Brin suggests that people who are all equally able to watch each other will be more forgiving of each other's small crimes, better able to stop each other's big crimes, and ultimately, better citizens.[1]

New technology makes transparency more important, but it is not a new concept. Brin follows the ideas of Karl Popper, a philosopher of the mid–20th century; and Justice Brandeis commented years ago that "sunshine is the best disinfectant." The United States now has open-government laws at all levels with "sunshine" provisions labeled in honor of Justice Brandeis' principle.[2]

Congress' own guide to requesting government information quotes James Madison:

> A popular Government without popular information or the means of acquiring it, is but a Prologue to a Farce or a Tragedy or perhaps both. Knowledge will forever govern ignorance, and a people who mean to be their own Governors, must arm themselves with the power knowledge gives.

First passed in 1966, the Freedom of Information Act (FOIA) made all federal records public except where the government could meet the burden of proving they should be closed. The FOIA received strengthening amendments and the Privacy Act was passed in 1974, during the era of outrage and reform that followed revelations about disreputable uses of government secrecy in the intelligence agencies and the Nixon White House. The Privacy Act allows citizens to request federal government information about themselves. It may be best known as the statute used in claiming access to one's own FBI file. Both the FOIA and the Privacy Act have been amended many times since their creation but their purpose of enforcing government openness remains the same. These laws have many local equivalents at the state and municipal levels.[3]

The Internet and electronic communications are further promoting some of the "transparency" goals Brin recommends. The main federal lawmaking and rulemaking documents have been publicly released for years, but until recently people who wanted to read them needed expensive subscriptions or access to a well-stocked research library. Now anyone with a computer and modem can follow a bill through Congress on THOMAS or a federal rulemaking process on GPO Access. (Many state legislatures have similar websites.)

Video cameras as a tool for transparency came into their own in March of 1991, when a bystander taped the vicious Los Angeles police beating of a now-famous suspect, Rodney King. Video-taping has become a common practice for people making many different points about law enforcement. Urban householders may videotape corner drug dealers to lobby for more police patrols; anti-brutality groups may videotape officers' sidewalk stops to encourage respectful policing; officers themselves may tape arrests to ensure they cannot later be falsely accused of misconduct. At political protests, video cameras appear in the hands of police, demonstrators, activist legal observers, and journalists.

Brin also points hopefully to the new phenomenon of private or nonprofit databases that offer the public a chance to look up elected representatives' campaign contributions.[4]

One official move in favor of transparency was a 2002 order from the Securities and Exchange Commission requiring the chiefs of certain large corporations to certify personally that their companies' financial statements were accurate.[5]

Noam Chomsky on Online Openness

I stay transparent. When I was organising resistance against the government I was open—that's the best protection. Somebody will be able to overcome any encryption technique you use! Our only weapons are truth, honesty, and openness.

—Noam Chomsky, controversial political writer and professor of linguistics at MIT, interviewed by Hamish Mackintosh, *The Guardian Online*, October 17, 2002. *www.guardian.co.uk/online/story/0,3605,812886,00.html*

Taking a somewhat related approach to openness, several states have passed "Megan's Laws," which require that convicted sex offenders, when released from prison, must place their addresses on a publicly distributed list. The laws are named after Megan Kanka, a seven-year-old murdered by a neighbor who had previously been convicted of sexual assaults against young girls.

The philosopher Amitai Etzioni, a "communitarian" who emphasizes individuals' responsibility to the group, discusses Megan's Laws among several case studies in his book *The Limits of Privacy*. He reluctantly opposes such laws, calling them insufficiently effective, but presents strong arguments on both sides of the issue. Etzioni notes that sex offenders are extremely likely to commit repeat offenses, so neighbors have good reason to be wary.[6]

The KlaasKids Foundation for Children, founded by the father of murder victim Polly Klaas, advocates for Megan's Laws and for fingerprinting children so they can be more easily found if abducted. Its website recommends a product called the Wherify GPS Personal Locator that links a child to the satellite Global Positioning System with a watchlike wristband. It promises, "Parents, whether at work, home, or traveling, can use the Internet or any phone to quickly identify their children's location within several feet, in about a minute. In the event of an emergency, either the child or parent can request an emergency 911 response. . . ."[7]

Openness is essential to public safety and good government.

The individual rights of free speech and privacy are both essential to democratic societies, and yet they often conflict with each other.

The First Amendment protects not only the right to speak, but the right to gather and publish information about others. Free speech would not be free if each speaker had to get

Should a reporter be able to find out who owns a car in order to write a news story?

In late September of 2001, a police officer uses a dog to search the University of Alabama—Birmingham locker room before a game. In the weeks after the terrorist attacks, security staff took special precautions all over the United States and ideas of personal privacy quickly began to change.

permission to quote or discuss every source of information. Within limits defined by the laws of intellectual property, defamation, right of privacy, and right of publicity, anyone has a right to say, print, or sell any fact about anyone else.

First Amendment values sometimes lead journalists to oppose privacy measures like the Driver's Privacy Protection Act. A recent journalism review article criticized government officials who withhold public records on security grounds, but added, "A greater threat, in the long run, comes from well-intentioned advocates of personal privacy. . . . The privacy movement has been under way for more than a decade, gathering public support and scoring some notable legislative successes. Driver's license information—a fundamental public record if ever there was one—has been restricted in many states. And basic medical news—such as the condition of a hospitalized crime or accident victim—may soon become unattainable."[8]

Meanwhile, in politics, a culture of competitive openness has developed since the "New Journalism" movement of the 1960s began telling unvarnished truths about public figures. At one time reporters quietly left out details that might make the public think badly of politicians. For example, the Washington press corps avoided mentioning that President Franklin Delano Roosevelt, a polio survivor, could walk only with difficulty and frequently used a wheelchair. Roosevelt himself wished to hide this fact, likely feeling that the voters of the 1930s and 1940s would not see him as the strong leader he was if they knew he was a "cripple."[9]

Now news reporters spare no details about politicians' health and habits. Candidates themselves often challenge each other to disclose personal information such as tax returns. Some have pushed each other to take drug tests as a way to show the public they have nothing to hide.

Sometimes the result is acceptance, not criticism. Physical disability is no longer a liability to a politician. Senators Robert Dole, Daniel Inouye, and Max Cleland all live with serious war wounds—and are more honored than stigmatized by the fact.

A number of political figures have admitted to past drug use or heavy drinking, and the resulting debate has increasingly emphasized their level of honesty rather than the embarrassing nature of their conduct. This trend began with admissions of addiction by First Lady Betty Ford in the 1970s and presidential candidate's wife Kitty Dukakis in the 1980s. In the 1990s Bill Clinton acknowledged trying marijuana but said he "didn't inhale." During the 2000 presidential campaign, George W. Bush was confronted four days before the

> **How important would it be to you to learn that a political candidate had used drugs 20 years ago?**
>
> **How relevant are private mistakes to a candidate's likely performance in public office?**

The Starr Report

One of the least inspiring episodes in recent American history is that of the Starr Report of 1998, which explored in lurid detail the nature of President Clinton's relationship with the intern Monica Lewinsky. A small sampling from the table of contents of that report should suffice to illustrate its idea of the privacy of a public official:

[. . .]

I. Nature of President Clinton's Relationship with Monica Lewinsky
   A. Introduction
   B. Evidence Establishing Nature of Relationship
      1. Physical Evidence
      2. Ms. Lewinsky's Statements
      3. Ms. Lewinsky's Confidants
      4. Documents
      5. Consistency and Corroboration
      [. . .]
   D. Emotional Attachment
   E. Conversations and Phone Messages
   F. Gifts
   G. Messages
   H. Secrecy
      1. Mutual Understanding
      2. Cover Stories
      3. Steps to Avoid Being Seen or Heard
      4. Ms. Lewinsky's Notes and Letters
      5. Ms. Lewinsky's Evaluation of Their Secrecy Efforts
II. 1995: Initial Sexual Encounters
   A. Overview of Monica Lewinsky's White House Employment
   B. First Meetings with the President
   C. November 15 Sexual Encounter
   D. November 17 Sexual Encounter
   E. December 31 Sexual Encounter
   [. . .]

—Office of Independent Counsel, "Referral to the
United States House of Representatives Pursuant to
Title 28, United States Code, §595(c)," September 9, 1998

election with a police report showing he had been arrested for driving under the influence of alcohol in 1976.[10]

Clinton faced many allegations of sexual misconduct during his presidency. As the resulting legal tangles became public, Americans probably learned more about his less glorious moments than about any president since Richard Nixon had to release his Oval Office tape recordings in 1974. Independent counsel Kenneth Starr's 1998 report gave painfully intimate details of Clinton's relationship with White House intern Monica Lewinsky. Nixon and Clinton were separately the subjects of court rulings saying that even the President cannot stop or postpone involvement in a court case against him.[11]

It may seem there ought to be a law against publishing too-personal details about famous people. Such reports frequently involve more prurient curiosity than public spirit. However, making too many rules about what people may find out and publish would have a "chilling effect" on free speech, with bad consequences for individual liberty and public accountability.

For example, it might seem reasonable to keep journalists from reporting on court filings in famous people's divorces. However, consider the papers recently filed by Jane Welch to divorce Jack Welch, retired CEO of General Electric. They revealed that GE, at the expense of its shareholders, was providing its former chief with some $2.5 million per year in benefits such as luxury housing and private jet service. The Securities and Exchange Commission promptly opened an informal investigation. Within days, Welch had volunteered under pressure to start paying for his perks. Although the news reports on the divorce papers did invade privacy, they also performed a public service.[12]

Should there be review boards to draw the line between the individual's right to privacy and the public's right to know?

How should such decisions be made?

AIDS drew sudden media attention and public concern in 1985 when film star Rock Hudson was revealed to be gay and seeking treatment for the disease. Gay community activists were glad for the help, but angered that the AIDS deaths of other gay men had not received as much attention.

Acceptance can be a better goal than secrecy.

In the 1980s, the AIDS epidemic was at its most deadly for gay men in the United States, and AIDS was widely thought of as a "gay disease." Some gay activists argued that the officials who controlled money for medical research and treatment would not make a serious effort to stop AIDS so long as being gay was considered shameful. They said lives depended on improving the public image of homosexuality.

The San Francisco Chronicle's Randy Shilts and Perry Land reported in 1985 that the movie star Rock Hudson, a Hollywood leading man with a conventionally masculine screen image, was actually gay and being tested for AIDS. Hudson acknowledged the AIDS testing through a spokesman, and then the reporters spoke with friends of Hudson's who agreed to be quoted saying he was gay. Hudson did in fact have AIDS, and died of it soon after.

In a sense, this was "outing" Hudson involuntarily—though at that time, a man with AIDS was often presumed gay, and Hudson's gayness was well known in Hollywood. The news of Hudson's diagnosis brought sudden mainstream media attention—and a sudden increase in research and treatment funding—to a disease that had needed it for years. Shilts wrote, "It took a square-jawed, heterosexually perceived actor like Rock Hudson to make AIDS something people could talk about."[13]

Gay activists have argued for years that honesty is the best policy on sexual orientation. In the U.S. military there have been ironic conflicting understandings on this point: one of the military's claimed reasons for opposing gay recruits has been that a gay service member could be blackmailed into revealing military secrets. But what threat of disclosure can scare a soldier who is already openly gay?

———•———•———•———

Our privacy may be gone, but at least it is possible to work for transparency. Unequal control over information is dangerous, but if everyone is equally able to watch everyone else, a loss of privacy need not mean a loss of fairness. Disclosures about people with bad records can protect others from physical or financial harm. Disclosures about politicians can help voters make the right decisions. Some reports about celebrities may seem too intrusive, but bad taste is better than censorship, and openness is more healthful than secrecy.

Some Kinds of Information Should Always Be Protected

S unshine makes a pleasant metaphor, but a life permanently exposed to others' eyes would be intolerable. Individual peace of mind depends on the "right to be let alone." People close the doors to bedrooms and bathrooms, not because they do anything surprising there, but because people have both a right and a psychological need to spend their undignified moments without an audience. Privacy of this kind is a basic characteristic of freedom, and one of the first that literal imprisonment takes away. Beyond the right to physical modesty, human beings have a right to live without a constant sense of being watched and judged.

David Brin uses the proverb that "people who live in glass houses shouldn't throw stones" to suggest that if we are all equally exposed to scrutiny we may forgive each other's failings. But Eugene (Evgeny) Zamiatin memorably saw the tyrannical side of "transparency." He was a Russian who had watched in distress as the Bolshevik Communist Party, having appeared to stand for freedom, instead invented total government in the years after 1917. Zamiatin's novel *We*, a lesser-known precursor of Orwell's *1984*, imagines a society whose people literally live in glass houses. They know they will be seen—and arrested—if they do anything rebellious or illogical. Some well-behaved citizens accept this arrangement. The story's hero does not.[1]

What would you think of a security measure that required all students in a school to carry transparent backpacks?

What about installing transparent lockers?

It would not serve any useful transparency or accountability purpose to drop the privacy protections for driver's license, health, and student records discussed in earlier chapters. That would only expose the subjects of the records to harm or embarrassment without helping at all to "keep them honest."

Even when people have committed serious crimes that deserve notoriety, public shaming is still not good policy. "Megan's Laws" may or may not protect children by telling their parents which neighbors to distrust. But such laws definitely have harmful effects on emotionally disturbed convicts emerging from prison. In *The Limits of Privacy*, Amitai Etzioni notes that several subjects of Megan's Law databases have been threatened and attacked after their release, and one man committed suicide, though possibly for unrelated reasons.[2]

At one time in the United States there was a notion that convicted criminals fully "paid their debt to society" by serving their assigned prison sentences. Megan's Laws inflict continuing punishment, although their stated purpose is to protect others. As Etzioni notes, the real question is whether people dangerous enough to belong on a warning list should be released into society at all. Etzioni even suggests that people judged capable of further sex crimes should be placed

Richard Smith of the Privacy Foundation discusses facial recognition software, which police can use to match faces in a crowd against databases of suspects. The accuracy of the technology is disputed, as are the ethical and legal implications of using it in public places such as sports stadiums.

in "protective custody" in a "guarded village or town" and kept there with tracking bracelets. Etzioni's proposals raise a difficult question: whether people should be punished for what they have done, or for what they might do. Is the answer different in cases of criminal insanity? What counts as insanity before the law? These are extremely difficult questions, worth a book in themselves.[3]

Perhaps an easier question to answer is whether children should be subjected to fingerprinting and satellite tracking for their own protection. If it is a tough moral decision whether to impose such requirements on adult ex-convicts, why impose them at all on children who have committed no crimes? Affixing locator wristbands to children may help parents feel better, but doesn't a child's everyday experience of being tracked by satellite have more to do with parents' assertions of control than with safety from criminal strangers? Is it healthy to teach future citizens of a free society that unauthorized travel is always out of the question? What would Tom Sawyer think?

It is only a short step from satellite-linked wristbands to the bizarre choice of a British couple, Wendy and Paul Duval, who decided to have their 11-year-old daughter implanted with a microchip "so that her movements can be traced if she is abducted."[4]

People should not be required to prove that they have nothing to hide.

Socially and legally, modern societies need to respect individuals' decisions about what they wish to disclose to the rest of the world. "Elizabeth" was willing to give birth to her son on live Internet video, and "Patti" to undergo public surgery, but they did not tell viewers their last names. It was their right to decide selectively, if unusually, what they would and would not make public.[5]

Chicago Cubs baseball star Sammy Sosa faced an intrusive challenge in the summer of 2002 from a *Sports Illustrated* columnist, Rick Reilly, who unexpectedly asked him to go to a medical lab and get tested for illegal drug use. Sosa told a Chicago reporter, "He was giving me an address to go to that place and take a test. I say to this guy, 'I will be first in line when Major League Baseball makes that decision.' But he wrote an address on a piece of paper and tried to hand it to me. I don't think this is the right way."[6]

Professing surprise at Sosa's anger, Reilly said, "Before last week, I thought Sammy was clean. He's never been hurt, which is a good sign . . . [b]ut now, after his reaction, I don't know. This puts some doubt in my mind."[7]

But *San Francisco Chronicle* columnist C.W. Nevius objected on civil libertarian grounds:

> So what's wrong with asking Sammy to offer up a few fluids for the good for the game? And, since you mention it, what's wrong with the Supreme Court ruling that any "students who participate in competitive after-school activities . . . may be required to test for drugs"? Well, because it isn't that simple. It begins with asking someone like Sosa to prove he isn't guilty. There was a senator named McCarthy who made quite a name for himself with that kind of logic. Why won't you say you aren't a Communist? If you won't deny it, doesn't that mean it is true?[8]

Senator Joseph McCarthy (R-Wisconsin) is best remembered for using his position in Congress to lead a campaign of investigation against civil servants and public figures whom he considered "disloyal" through alleged sympathy with Communism. His campaign began in 1950 and gathered strength until 1954, when his attempt to investigate the Army collapsed in a scandal about the furtive behavior of his own staff. The postwar period that is sometimes called the McCarthy Era saw political investigations by McCarthy's Senate committee, the House Un-American Activities Committee (HUAC), and by legislators in states such as California whose

Is refusing to take a drug test a sign of guilt?

Senator Joseph P. McCarthy (R-Wisconsin) holds a whispered consultation with his chief counsel, Roy Cohn, during the Army–McCarthy hearings in April of 1954. Despite the "innocent until proven guilty" ideal of the American justice system, the proceedings of the House Un-American Activities Committee often began with the assumption of guilt.

stated goal was to expose and disgrace Communists. They wanted to aim their own kind of "sunshine"—the hostile public gaze—at people they felt had something to hide. There are many who remember this campaign as being anything but healthy for the nation.[9]

During that same period, a separate legal dispute emerged over the privacy of membership lists. It began in 1951, when the National Association for the Advancement of Colored People (NAACP) opened a regional office in the racially segregated state of Alabama to advocate for the rights of African-American residents. State attorneys sued the organization and tried to get it thrown out of the state, saying it had failed to register with local authorities under laws governing out-of-state corporations.

Do the rules for forming clubs or other organizations in schools and colleges respect the right of free association?

Should they?

In the course of the lawsuit, a state court ordered the NAACP to hand over its membership list. In 1950s Alabama, being known to state officials as an NAACP member could have caused a person many problems, including physical danger. The organization's leadership refused, and the case found its way to the Supreme Court. There, Thurgood Marshall, the future Supreme Court Justice, was among the attorneys arguing that NAACP members had a constitutional right not to have their membership disclosed to the state.

In 1958 the Supreme Court agreed with the NAACP, saying the membership lists were protected from disclosure under the Fourteenth Amendment's Due Process Clause, which required state governments to respect First Amendment rights.[10]

Justice Douglas, commenting later in *Griswold v. Connecticut*, said the decision protected "freedom to associate and privacy in one's associations"—a First Amendment privacy right.[11]

"Sunshine" is still inflicted abusively. A Florida law now provides that if a woman wants to give up her child for adoption and is not certain of the father, she must publish a

FROM THE BENCH

From *NAACP v. Alabama*, 357 U.S. 449 (1958)

... Effective advocacy of both public and private points of view, particularly controversial ones, is undeniably enhanced by group association, as this Court has more than once recognized by remarking upon the close nexus between the freedoms of speech and assembly.... It is beyond debate that freedom to engage in association for the advancement of beliefs and ideas is an inseparable aspect of the "liberty" assured by the Due Process Clause of the Fourteenth Amendment, which embraces freedom of speech....

newspaper notice describing every man who could possibly be the father. In Iowa, anti-abortion organizations publicize photographs and video footage of women who enter abortion clinics. Worse, in the fall of 2002, Iowa authorities investigating the murder of an unidentified newborn infant obtained a court order telling a local Planned Parenthood office to disclose the results of all its patients' pregnancy tests for nine months of operation. Planned Parenthood contested the decision.[12]

Even the famous have a right to be let alone.

The public pursuit of celebrities can range from deadly serious, as in the case of Rebecca Shaeffer's murder, to the merely upsetting. Into the latter category falls the case of A.J. Weberman, an angry former fan of the singer/songwriter Bob Dylan who practiced what he called "garbology"— rooting through Dylan's trash cans for unflattering material to publish.[13]

What is the difference between journalism and stalking?

Even mainstream celebrity journalism can involve strange gamesmanship, as in Jan McGirk's tale of "staking out" a Mexican resort where actor Freddie Prinze, Jr.

was to marry Sarah Michelle Gellar, the star of TV's *Buffy the Vampire Slayer*:

> First we had to confirm exactly when and where it was happening, although all the participants were sworn to secrecy and the guests were not told their destination. . . . The wedding party had booked all hotel rooms and villas within view of the cliff-top ceremony at Punto Careyes. . . . The scramble to pinpoint Gellar soon resembled one of Buffy's cheesy television plots. . . . Some of us definitely deserved danger money. Crocodiles lurked in the mangrove lagoons adjacent to Buffy's beach. The jungle-clad cliffs required a machete and heavy-duty mosquito repellant. . . .[14]

Perhaps some stars make themselves inaccessible for reasons of egotism as well as privacy. But don't citizens have a right to decide who isn't invited to their wedding? There is a certain amount of hypocrisy involved in "right to know" arguments about celebrities. People who would not welcome gate-crashers at their own parties may cheerfully read uninvited visitors' accounts of celebrity weddings.

Barbra Streisand's son, Jason Gould, told a reporter in 2000, "When I was a kid I couldn't go anywhere without photographers in our face. . . . I don't like cameras snapping in my face. It's like being attacked."[15]

Intrusions like this indicate the need to draw lines between free speech and privacy rights. Although U.S. law protects more speech than most other industrialized countries, it does offer some protection against abusive publicity. Courts ordinarily conceal the surnames of parties under 18, and all but the most serious juvenile court records are sealed to protect the subjects' adult reputations. Most newspapers suppress the names of rape victims—a traditional practice that is, however, controversial because of the argument that it falsely suggests that rape is something the victim should be ashamed of.

Victims of slander and libel (spoken or written falsehoods that damage reputation) can sue for compensation. For people victimized by true or partly true statements about them, U.S. law traditionally recognizes four privacy torts—that is, legal theories the victims can use to claim compensation for injury. Not all states recognize exactly the same privacy torts, but in their classic form they are:

- "Unreasonable intrusion upon the seclusion of another,"

- "Appropriation of the other's name or likeness,"

- "Unreasonable publicity given to the other's private life," and

- "Publicity that unreasonably places the other in a false light before the public."[16]

If Dylan had sued the "garbologist," he might have alleged "unreasonable intrusion upon seclusion" and "unreasonable publicity given to private life." Court decisions sometimes observe that people who work hard to become famous cannot complain too much if people want to watch them. In cases involving publication of private facts, important legal issues include whether the alleged victim was a "public figure," whether the information was obtained legally, and whether the material reported is newsworthy or of public concern.

> **How would you feel if someone angry with you went through your garbage?**

"Appropriation of name or likeness" is a tort violating the "right of publicity." The right of publicity would, for example, allow an actress to stop a magazine from publishing her photo in an advertisement, though the magazine could still publish the photo without her permission as part of a news report.

"False light" is closely related in law to defamation (known as "libel" if written, "slander" if spoken). Defamation is a falsehood that hurts the victim's reputation, while "false light" is a knowingly or recklessly publicized false implication that is "highly offensive to a reasonable person," whether or not the person's reputation is harmed.[17]

Invaded privacy can victimize public heroes.

Journalism textbooks tell the sad story of Oliver Sipple, a gay former Marine who saved President Gerald Ford's life in 1975. As Ford left a San Francisco hotel, Sipple spotted an assassin, Sara Jane Moore, aiming a gun. He struck her hand and caused the shot to miss.

Gay activists, including Harvey Milk, complained that Ford was slow to extend proper thanks because Sipple was gay. (In 2001, Ford told an interviewer, "I don't know where anyone got the crazy idea I was prejudiced and wanted to exclude gays.")[18]

Sipple himself would not discuss his sexual orientation

FROM THE BENCH

From *Sipple v. Chronicle Publishing, Inc.,* 154 Cal.App. 3d. 1040, 1049 (Cal. 1st Dist., 1984)

... [T]he record shows that the publications were not motivated by a morbid and sensational prying into appellant's private life but rather were prompted by legitimate political considerations, i.e., to dispel the false public opinion that gays were timid, weak and unheroic figures and to raise the equally important political question whether the President of the United States entertained a discriminatory attitude or bias against a minority group such as homosexuals. ...

with reporters, but, at the activists' urging, *The San Francisco Chronicle* and then the national press carried reports strongly implying he was gay. Sipple was openly gay in San Francisco, but he had not told his conservative parents in Detroit. They were shocked to read this in the newspapers, and his mother never spoke to him again.

Sipple sued several papers unsuccessfully for invasion of privacy. One 1984 California court decision threw out his claim, saying the facts published were not private, because Sipple had openly partici- **Which side in** pated in gay political and cultural events, ***Sipple* was right?** and they were newsworthy because, by saving the President's life, he had involuntarily become a public figure. In other words, Sipple's heroism was too important for a free press to let him alone.[19, 20]

Some invasions of privacy do not have the "transparency" effect of promoting honesty and safety—they only violate individuals' right to decide what information to disclose. Demands for openness can be vindictive and hypocritical. There are good reasons why even the United States, with its strong free speech protections, allows victims of unfair publicity to sue for defamation and invasion of privacy.

Drawing Lines

The main privacy debates involve drawing lines: between police and individuals; between journalists and subjects; between businesses and consumers. Because of cultural and political change, these lines are drawn in different places than in the past. And while it has always been important to control what is disclosed, now it is also important to prevent information collected for one purpose from being unfairly used for another.

It is hard to know whether individual Americans have more or less privacy now than in 1791. Eighteenth-century America was innocent of wiretapping, but it tolerated profound inequalities, neglected procedural rights, and

Why does the Bill of Rights not mention privacy specifically?

What laws need to be made to protect privacy— and how far should the government be involved in protecting it?

did little about abuse within households. Government intrusion was firmly banned from the home, but laws influenced by social and religious prejudice restricted family formation decisions in ways that modern courts have rejected as intolerable.

When the Supreme Court invalidated a series of family formation laws on privacy grounds in the later 20th century, it did so on venerable principles, but it was also acting in the context of changed social attitudes about religion and family life.

One of the most important cases of this type was the 1965 birth control decision of *Griswold v. Connecticut*.[1] A group of activists were arrested under a state morals law for helping married couples to obtain contraceptives. Justice Douglas' opinion picked up Justice Brandeis' idea of the "right to be let alone" and used it to identify a constitutional right to family privacy. Douglas argued that the right to privacy is a basic assumption underlying the Bill of Rights, though privacy is not mentioned in so many words.

Other important cases protecting family or household formation include the 1942 case of *Skinner v. Oklahoma*,

FROM THE BENCH

From *Griswold v. Connecticut*, 381 U.S. 479 (1965)

...Various guarantees create zones of privacy. The right of association contained in the penumbra of the First Amendment is one, as we have seen. The Third Amendment in its prohibition against the quartering of soldiers "in any house" in time of peace without the consent of the owner is another facet of that privacy. The Fourth Amendment explicitly affirms the "right of the people to be secure in their persons, houses, papers, and effects, against unreasonable searches and seizures." The Fifth Amendment in its Self-Incrimination Clause enables the citizen to create a zone of privacy which government may not force him to surrender to his detriment. The Ninth Amendment provides: "The enumeration in the Constitution, of certain rights, shall not be construed to deny or disparage others retained by the people."

upholding the right of convicts to refuse sterilization; *Loving v. Virginia*, in 1967, on the right of interracial couples to marry; *Eisenstadt v. Baird*, in 1972, allowing contraceptives to be sold to unmarried people; *Roe v. Wade*, in 1973, the landmark case that established the right to abortion, using a theory based on the *Griswold* version of a constitutional right to privacy; *Carey v. Population Services International*, in 1977, on the right to distribute contraceptives to minors, *Moore v. City of East Cleveland*, in 1977, on the right of grandparents to live with their grandchildren, and *Zablocki v. Redhail*, in 1978, on the right of a parent already under a child support order to marry without court permission.

Two newer cases have narrowed the law on issues of household formation: *Bowers v. Hardwick*, in 1986, upheld a Georgia law against consensual sexual relations between gay men, and *Planned Parenthood v. Casey*, in 1992, allowed states to impose certain restrictions on the right to abortion so long as it was not banned outright.[2]

Just as social change drove changes in family law, technological change is driving changes in information law. It is perhaps too soon to tell whether the attacks of September of 2001 have created a genuinely new era in politics, but the year following the attacks definitely did cause massive changes in the law of privacy rights and public safety. The frequent reports of investigations and detentions, and the emergence of federal court challenges to assertions of executive-branch authority, placed the police powers of the federal government at issue in a manner the United States had not seen since the 1970s.

Possibly future readers will look back on the early 21st century as the beginning of a period in which surveillance and data manipulation provided American institutions with new power bases—or it may be remembered as a kind of "Wild West" period when new technologies had not yet been tamed by an indignant public and their legislators.

Technological innovation does not, however, seem likely

Police closed-circuit TV cameras are now a common sight in Britain's urban public spaces. Police departments are beginning to use this method in some U.S. cities, too, including Washington, D.C.—which raises the obvious questions of who is watching and what will be done with the information thus gathered.

to change the fact that democratic freedoms depend on maintaining democratically chosen separations—for example, the separation of powers among the executive branch, Congress, and the courts; separation between foreign spying and domestic policing; separation between public and private databases;

separations among privately created databases whose com-
bination would invade privacy; and separations between the use
of data for its intended purpose (health care, credit card billing)
and the use of data for other purposes (marketing, insurance
policy decisions).

Separations create inefficiency, but inefficiency is essential
to democracy and, especially, to privacy.

Maybe privacy really is an impractical old-fashioned luxury
we can learn to live without. Maybe the best we can hope for is
David Brin's "transparency"—equal lack of privacy for all.

Or maybe we are simply in a period of adjustment, when
the complete loss of privacy seems possible only because we
have not yet made the right rules for living comfortably in a
technologically and politically new world.

———•————————•————————•———

Law changes with society: changed ideas about religion and the
family led to a changed Supreme Court definition of household
privacy. What hasn't changed in privacy law, and in democracy
generally, is the need to draw lines—to maintain separations
between what can and can't be disclosed, and between one kind
of disclosure and another. This need is especially important
given the political and technological changes that are exposing
individual people's lives to ever-increasing scrutiny.

Defining and Valuing the Right to Privacy

1 See, e.g., *Mapp v. Ohio*, 367 U.S. 643 (1961); *Yick Wo v. Hopkins*, 118 U.S. 356 (1886); and, e.g., *Shaughnessy v. Mezei*, 345 U.S. 206 (1953); *Plyler v. Doe*, 457 U.S. 202 (1982); and *U.S. v. Verdugo-Urquidez*, 494 U.S. 259 (1990).

2 Hendrik Hartog, *Man and Wife in America: A History*, Harvard University Press, 2000; Sally E. Hadden, *Slave Patrols: Law and Violence in Virginia and the Carolinas*, Harvard University Press, 2001.

3 Samuel D. Warren and Louis D. Brandeis, "The Right to Privacy," *Harvard Law Review* 4(1890):193.

4 *Olmstead v. United States*, 277 U.S. 438, 478 (1928).

5 *Katz v. United States*, 389 U.S. 347 (1967).

Point: Not Everyone Can Be Safely "Let Alone"

1 Library of Congress: THOMAS, "Legislation Related to the Attack of September 11, 2001," *thomas.loc.gov/home/terrorleg.htm*.

2 Richard Posner, "The Law: Security Versus Civil Liberties," *The Atlantic Monthly* (December 2001).

3 Zachary Coile, "Ashcroft Stands His Ground: Civil Liberties Focus of Judiciary Committee Testimony," *The San Francisco Chronicle* (December 7, 2001).

4 Jeff Jacoby, "Airport Security Is Just Too PC," reprinted in *The San Francisco Chronicle* (June 24, 2002).

5 Attorney General John Ashcroft, Remarks, Press Briefing with FBI Director Robert Mueller, FBI Headquarters, September 17, 2001, available online at *www.usdoj.gov/ag/speeches/2001/0917pressbriefingfbi.htm*.

6 John Solomon, "Terror Network Calls Tracked by U.S.," Associated Press (September 15, 2002).

7 Homeland Security Act of 2002, Public Law 107–296; Carrie Kirby, "Personal Privacy Takes Alarming Hit, Critics Say," The San Francisco Chronicle (November 20, 2002); Edward Epstein, "Senate Passes Security Bill," The San Francisco Chronicle (November 20, 2002); "Homeland Security Bill on Verge of Passage; CDT Pursues Oversight Strategy," Center for Democracy and Technology (November 19, 2002), available online at *www.cdt.org/wiretap/021119homelandsecurity.shtml*.

8 "Total Information Awareness," editorial, *The Washington Post* (November 16, 2002):A20; remarks of Sen. Bill Nelson (November 18, 2002), *Congressional Record* S11250–S11251, excerpted in "Grave Questions of Invasion of Privacy," Salon.com (November 26, 2002), *www.salon.com/news/feature/2002/11/26/nelson_speech/index.html*.

9 Wayne R. LaFave, *Search and Seizure: A Treatise on the Fourth Amendment*, 3d ed. with pocket part, West, 1996. See vol. 2, ch. 4 generally and pp. 438, 445.

10 *Terry v. Ohio*, 392 U.S. 1 (1968).

11 *Weeks v. United States*, 232 U.S. 383 (1914); *Mapp v. Ohio*, 367 U.S. 643 (1961).

12 David Firestone, "After Shootings, Nation's Schools Add to Security," *The New York Times* (August 13, 1999):A1.

13 Available online at *www.cdc.gov/nccdphp/dash/yrbs/index.htm*.

14 Mark H. Moore, Carol V. Petrie, Anthony A. Braga, and Breanda L. McLaughlin (eds.), *Deadly Lessons: Understanding Lethal School Violence*, National Academy Press, 2002, p. 300.

15 Lisa Fernandez, "Heavy Lessons to Learn: Students Bear Brunt of Locker Bans in Weighty Knapsacks," *The San Francisco Chronicle* (February 9, 1999).

16 Darcia Harris Bowman, "Student Tips Called Key to Avert Violence," *Education Week* (March 14, 2001); Melissa L. Gilbert, "'Time-Out' for Student Threats: Imposing a Duty to Protect on School Officials," *UCLA Law Review* 49(2002):917.

17 *New Jersey v. T.L.O.*, 469 U.S. 325 (1985); LaFave, vol. 4, §10.11 generally and pp. 808–811.

18 Gilbert; *Tarasoff v. Regents of University of California*, 17 Cal.3d 425 (1976).

19 Paul K. Legler, "The Impact of Welfare Reform on the Child Support Enforcement System," in J. Thomas Oldham and Marygold S. Melli (eds.), *Child Support: The Next Frontier*, University of Michigan Press, 2000, p. 47.

20 Public Law 104–193 §333; 42 U.S.C. §654; 7 U.S.C. §2015; 42 U.S.C. §666.

21 See, e.g., "Employee Privacy: Computer-Use Monitoring Practices and Policies of Selected Companies," U.S. General Accounting Office (GAO), Report No. GAO-02-717, September 2002 (October 28, 2002), available online at *www.gao.gov/new.items/d02717.pdf*.

22 *Skinner v. Railway Labor Executives Assn.*, 489 U.S. 602 (1989); *National Treasury Employees Union v. Von Raab*, 489 U.S. 656 (1989).

23 *Vernonia School District 47J v. Acton*, 515 U.S. 646 (1995).

24 *Board of Education of Independent School District No. 92 of Pottawatomie County v. Earls*, U.S. Supreme Court, June 27, 2002, docket no. 01–332, unofficial text available online at *supct.law.cornell.edu/supct/html/01-332.ZS.html*.

25 *Ibid.*, quoting *Griffin v. Wisconsin*, 483 U.S. 868 (1987).

26 "Convicted by Juries, Exonerated by Science: Case Studies in the Use of DNA Evidence to Establish Innocence After Trial," U.S. Department of Justice: Office of Justice Programs: National Institute of Justice (June 1996), available online at *www.ncjrs.org/pdffiles/dnaevid.pdf*.

Counterpoint: Too Much Official Invasion of Privacy Harms the Public Interest

1 Benjamin Franklin, quoted in John Bartlett, *Familiar Quotations*, 10th ed., 1919.

2 Juvenal, *Satires* VI, ll. 347–348: "*Quis custodiet ipsos custodes?*"

3 James Morton Smith, *Freedom's Fetters: The Alien and Sedition Laws and American Civil Liberties*, Cornell University Press, 1956, 1967.

4 William Rehnquist, *All the Laws But One: Civil Liberties in Wartime*, Knopf/Borzoi, 1998; Paul L. Murphy, *World War I and the Origin of Civil Liberties in the United States*, Norton, 1979, pp. 90–91.

5 Louis F. Post, *The Deportations Delirium of Nineteen-Twenty: A Personal Narrative of an Historic Official Experience*, Charles H. Kerr, 1923; reprint Da Capo Press, 1970.

6 Lawson Fusao Inada (ed.), *Only What We Could Carry: The Japanese American Internment Experience*, California Historical Society/Heyday Books, 2000; Michelle T. Maki, Harry H.L. Kitano, and S. Megan Berthold (eds.), *Achieving the Impossible Dream: How Japanese Americans Obtained Redress*, University of Illinois Press, 1999; *Minoru Yasui v. United States*, 320 U.S. 115 (1943); *Kiyoshi Hirabayashi v. United States*, 320 U.S. 81 (1943); *Toyosaburo Korematsu v. United States*, 323 U.S. 214 (1944); *Ex Parte Mitsuye Endo*, 323 U.S. 283 (1944).

7 The American Civil Liberties Union (ACLU), "The Dangers of Domestic Spying by Federal Law Enforcement: A Case Study on FBI Surveillance of Dr. Martin Luther King," available online

through *www.aclu.org/SafeandFree/ SafeandFreeMain.cfm;* "Final Report of the Senate Select Committee to Study Governmental Operations with Respect to Intelligence Activities," 94th Cong., 2d Sess., Rept. No. 94-755 (1976) ("Church Committee Report").

8 Jon Carroll, "No Reason to Panic! We Are Not in Control!" *The San Francisco Chronicle* (July 10, 2002):D10.

9 Amnesty International, "Amnesty International's Concerns Regarding Post–September 11 Detentions in the USA," *www.amnestyusa.org/usacrisis/ 9.11.detentions2.pdf* (released March 14, 2002); Steve Fainaru, "U.S. Deported 131 Pakistanis in Secret Airlift," *The Washington Post* (July 10, 2002):A01; *Detroit Free Press v. Ashcroft*, 6th Cir. Court of Appeals, docket no. 02–1437, August 26, 2002, available online at *pacer.ca6.uscourts.gov/opinions.pdf/02a0 291p-06.pdf.*

12 "Total Information Awareness," editorial, *The Washington Post* (November 16, 2002):A20; remarks of Sen. Bill Nelson (November 18, 2002), *Congressional Record* S11250–S11251, excerpted in "Grave Questions of Invasion of Privacy," Salon.com (November 26, 2002), *www.salon.com/news/feature/ 2002/11/26/nelson_speech/index.html.*

11 The American Civil Liberties Union (ACLU), "The Dangers of Domestic Spying by Federal Law Enforcement: A Case Study on FBI Surveillance of Dr. Martin Luther King," appendix, available online through *www.aclu.org/ SafeandFree/SafeandFreeMain.cfm;* ACLU legislative analysis, USA PATRIOT Act, November 1, 2001, *www.aclu.org/congress/l110101a.html;* FISA, 50 U.S.C. §§1804, 1823; USA PATRIOT Act, Public Law 107–56, §218.

12 *California v. Acevedo*, 500 U.S. 565, 582–583 (1991) (Scalia, J., concurring).

13 Mark H. Moore, Carol V. Petrie, Anthony A. Braga, and Breanda L. McLaughlin (eds.), *Deadly Lessons: Understanding Lethal School Violence*, National Academy Press, 2002, pp. 300–301.

14 Lisa Fernandez, "Heavy Lessons to Learn: Students Bear Brunt of Locker Bans in Weighty Knapsacks," *The San Francisco Chronicle* (February 9, 1999).

15 Darcia Harris Bowman, "Student Tips Called Key to Avert Violence," *Education Week* (March 14, 2001).

16 Jerome Beigler, "Psychiatric Confidentiality and the American Legal System: An Ethical Conflict," in Sidney Bloch and Paul Chodoff (eds.), *Psychiatric Ethics*, Oxford University Press, 1981, p. 229; Toksoz Karasu, "Ethical Aspects of Psychotherapy," in the same collection, pp. 105–106.

17 See California Business and Professions Code §6068(e).

18 Kate Millett, *Sexual Politics*, University of Illinois Press, 2000, pp. 164–174.

19 *Moodian v. County of Alameda Social Services Agency*, U.S. District Court, Northern District of California, No. C 01–1546 BZ, order, June 3, 2002, available online through *www.cand.uscourts.gov; Bryant-Bruce v. Vanderbilt University, Inc.*, 974 F. Supp. 1127 (M.D. Tenn., 1997); Chuck Squatriglia, "Ruling Hinders Social Workers: Investigation Limits for Emotional Abuse," *The San Francisco Chronicle* (June 10, 2002).

20 Mimi Abramovitz, *Regulating the Lives of Women: Social Welfare Policy from Colonial Times to the Present*, South End Press, 1996, pp. 313–326.

21 Jessica Pearson and Esther Ann Griswold, "Child Support Policies and Domestic Violence: A Preliminary Look at Client Experiences with Good Cause Exemptions to Child Support

Cooperation Requirements," Center for Policy Research (January 1997), available online at *www.acf.dhhs.gov/programs/cse/rpt/mofc/3domviol.htm*; Jessica Pearson, Nancy Thoennes, and Esther Ann Griswold, "Child Support and Domestic Violence: The Victims Speak Out," Center for Policy Research (March 6, 1998), available online at *www.acf.hhs.gov/programs/cse/rpt/mofc/4victims.htm*.

22 Ray Ginger, *Altgeld's America: The Lincoln Ideal Versus Changing Realities*, Franklin Watts/New Viewpoints, 1973, pp. 145–163.

23 Michel Foucault, *Discipline and Punish: The Birth of the Prison*, trans. Alan Sheridan, Random House/Vintage, 1995, p. 200; Mike Davis, *City of Quartz: Excavating the Future in Los Angeles*, Vintage, 1992, pp. 243–244.

24 Barbara Ehrenreich, *Nickel and Dimed: On (Not) Getting By in America*, Metropolitan, 2001, pp. 58–59.

25 The 1997 science fiction film *Gattaca* provides an interesting thought-experiment on the societal implications of genetic mapping.

26 Barbara Ehrenreich, *Nickel and Dimed: On (Not) Getting By in America*, Metropolitan, 2001, pp. 128.

27 Harriet Chiang, "Supreme Court Broadens Drug Testing at Schools—Bay Area Districts Demur," *The San Francisco Chronicle* (June 28, 2002): A1.

Point: Civilized Life Requires the Exchange of Information

1 Henry T. Greely makes this point in "Trusted Systems and Medical Records: Lowering Expectations," *Stanford Law Review* 52(2000):1585, 1588.

2 Joel Garreau, "Like the Bee, This Evolving Species Buzzes and Swarms," *The Washington Post* (July 31, 2002):C01.

3 *Bartnicki v. Vopper*, 532 U.S. 514 (2001); *Edwards v. State Farm Ins. Co.*, 833 F.2d 535 (1987); John Wesley Hall, *Professional Responsibility of the Criminal Lawyer*, 2d ed., Clark Boardman Callaghan, 1996, pp. 883–884.

4 See, e.g., RealNetworks "Privacy Policy," *www.realnetworks.com/company/privacy/index.html*.

5 "Northwestern Memorial Selects Data Mining Vendor," press release, Health Data Management (October 24, 2001), available online through *www.healthdatamanagement.com*; "iD Solutions (TM) Helps Kaiser Permanente Adapt Its Business and Save Lives," online brochure, Cincom Systems, Inc., 2001, available online through *www.cincom.com*.

6 Jonathan Zittrain, "What the Publisher Can Teach the Patient: Intellectual Property and Privacy in an Era of Trusted Privication," *Stanford Law Review* 52(2000):1201, 1241.

7 Jessica Litman, "Information Privacy/Information Property," *Stanford Law Review* 52(2000):1283.

8 *Reno v. Condon*, 528 U.S. 141 (2000); DPPA, 18 U.S.C. §§2721–2725; Jonathan Zittrain, "What the Publisher Can Teach the Patient: Intellectual Property and Privacy in an Era of Trusted Privication," *Stanford Law Review* 52(2000):1234.

9 18 U.S.C. §2710 *et seq.*; Jessica Litman, "Information Privacy/Information Property," *Stanford Law Review* 52(2000):1283, 1305.

10 See 15 U.S.C. ch. 94, "Privacy"; U.S. Federal Trade Commission, "Pretexting: Your Personal Information Revealed," *www.ftc.gov/bcp/conline/pubs/credit/pretext.htm*.

11 Anita L. Allen, "Gender and Privacy," *Stanford Law Review* 52(2000):1175, 1188–1191; *www.jennicam.org*.

Counterpoint: Institutions and Businesses Exploit Personal Information Unfairly

1 Polly Sprenger, "Sun on Privacy: 'Get Over It,'" *Wired* (January 26, 1999), *www.wired.com/news/politics/0,1283,17538,00.html*; Dan Fost, "Online Disguises from Prying Eyes: New Software Helps Keep Internet Activities Private," *The San Francisco Chronicle* (September 23, 1999).

2 Faye Flam, "Your Brain May Soon Be Used Against You: The Last Refuge of Secrets and Lies, the Brain, May Be About to Reveal All," *The Philadelphia Inquirer* (October 29, 2002).

3 A. Michael Froomkin, "The Death of Privacy?" *Stanford Law Review* 52(2000):1461, 1468–1472, 1471, n.30. For an interesting fictional riff on "data mining," see William Gibson's novel *Idoru*.

4 Benny Evangelista, "Ruling a Triumph for Music Industry: Internet Providers Can't Shield Downloaders," *The San Francisco Chronicle* (January 22, 2003); Memorandum Opinion and Order, *In Re: Verizon Internet Services, Inc.,* Judge John D. Bates, U.S. District Court for the District of Columbia, Civil Action No. 02-MS-0323, January 21, 2003, *www.dcd.uscourts.gov/02-ms-323.pdf*; "Nation's Big Three Consumer Reporting Agencies Agree to Pay $2.5 Million to Settle FTC Charges of Violating Fair Credit Reporting Act," press release, U.S. Federal Trade Commission (January 13, 2000), available online at *www.ftc.gov/opa/2000/01/busysignal.htm*; "How to Dispute Credit Report Errors," U.S. Federal Trade Commission, *www.ftc.gov/bcp/conline/pubs/credit/crdtdis.htm*; 15 U.S.C. §1681 *et seq.*; "Identity Fraud Information: Maine Secretary of State," *www.state.me.us/sos/IDfraud.htm*.

5 EPIC, DoubleClick U.S. Federal Trade Commission complaint, *www.epic.org/privacy/internet/ftc/DCLK_complaint.pdf*.

6 U.S. Federal Trade Commission closing letter to DoubleClick (January 22, 2001), *www.ftc.gov/os/closings/staff/doubleclick.pdf*; EPIC, "Cookies," *www.epic.org/privacy/internet/cookies/*.

7 Robert Vamosi, "What Is Spyware?" ZDNet Reviews (June 28, 2001); Chris Wenham, "A Law to Protect Spyware," Salon.com (April 26, 2002), *www.salon.com/tech/feature/2002/04/26/hollings_spyware/*.

8 U.S. Federal Trade Commission Complaint, "In the Matter of Microsoft Corporation" (August 2002), available online at *www.ftc.gov/os/2002/08/microsoftcmp.pdf*; "Microsoft Settles FTC Charges Alleging False Security and Privacy Promises," press release, U.S. Federal Trade Commission (August 8, 2002), available online at *www.ftc.gov/opa/2002/08/microsoft.htm*; Joe Wilcox, "Microsoft Shores Up Passport Security," ZDNet (September 3, 2002), available online through *www.zdnet.com*.

9 Laura Flanders, "Librarians Under Siege," *The Nation* (August 5, 2002); American Library Association, "FBI in Your Library," *www.ala.org/alaorg/oif/fbiinyourlibrary.html*; Seth Rosenfeld, "Patriot Act's Scope, Secrecy Ensnare Innocent, Critics Say," *The San Francisco Chronicle* (September 8, 2002).

10 The Homeland Security Act of 2002, Public Law 107–296, §880; Dan Eggen, "Under Fire, Justice Shrinks TIPS Program," *The Washington Post* (August 10, 2002):A1.

11 Michele Kayal, "The Societal Costs of Surveillance," *The New York Times* (July 26, 2002).

12 Hannah Arendt, *The Origins of Totalitarianism*, Harcourt Brace Jovanovich, 1979, p. 323.

93

13 Peter Skerry, *Counting On the Census?: Race, Group Identity, and the Evasion of Politics*, Brookings Institution, 2000, p. 34; Thomas S. Mayer, "Privacy and Confidentiality Research and the U.S. Census Bureau," U.S. Bureau of the Census, Statistical Research Division, Research Report Series (Survey Methodology #2002–01), p. 24.

14 Thomas S. Mayer, "Privacy and Confidentiality Research and the U.S. Census Bureau," U.S. Bureau of the Census, Statistical Research Division, Research Report Series (Survey Methodology #2002–01), pp. 4–5.

15 *Congressional Record* (April 3, 2000): H1663.

16 U.S. Department of Health and Human Services, press releases of June 3 and August 9, 2002, available online at *www.hhs.gov/news/press/2002pres/hipaa.html* and *www.hhs.gov/news/press/2002pres/20020809a.html*; "Standards for Privacy of Individually Identifiable Health Information: Final Rule," 67 FR 53182 (August 14, 2002).

17 See 20 U.S.C. §1232g; 20 U.S.C. §1232h; 8 U.S.C. §1372; and especially 34 CFR Part 99; David A. Banisar, "Privacy of Education Records," Electronic Privacy Information Center, 1994, available online at *www.epic.org/privacy/education/school.html*; *Gonzaga University v. Doe*, U.S. Supreme Court, June 20, 2002, docket no. 01–679.

Point: A Free Society Depends on the Right to Learn and Share Information

1 David Brin, *The Transparent Society: Will Technology Force Us to Choose Between Privacy and Freedom?*, Addison-Wesley, 1998.

2 E.g., "The Government in the Sunshine Act," Public Law 94–409, 5 U.S.C. §551 *et seq.*; "A Citizen's Guide on Using the Freedom of Information Act and the Privacy Act of 1974 to Request Government Records: First Report by the Committee on Government Reform," Cong. Report No. 107–371 (March 12, 2002), available online via *www.thomas.gov* and *www.access.gpo.gov*.

3 "A Citizen's Guide on Using the Freedom of Information Act and the Privacy Act of 1974 to Request Government Records: First Report by the Committee on Government Reform," Cong. Report No. 107–371 (March 12, 2002), available online via *www.thomas.gov* and *www.access.gpo.gov*; The Freedom of Information Act, 5 U.S.C. §552; the Privacy Act of 1974, 5 U.S.C. §552a. Madison comment quoted on p. 2 of "A Citizen's Guide," citing Madison's letter to W.T. Barry, August 4, 1822, in G.P. Hunt (ed.), *The Writings of James Madison*, 1910, vol. IX, p. 103.

4 See, for example, *www.opensecrets.org*.

5 U.S. Securities and Exchange Commission, "Order Requiring the Filing of Sworn Statements Pursuant to Section 21(a)(1) of the Securities Exchange Act of 1934," file no. 4:460, OMB no. 3235–0569 (June 27, 2002), available online at *www.sec.gov/rules/other/4-460.htm*.

6 Amitai Etzioni, *The Limits of Privacy*, Perseus Books Group/Basic Books, 1999, pp. 45, 50–53.

7 KlaasKids Foundation, "Legislation: Megan's Law," available online at *www.klaaskids.org/pg-legmeg.htm*; "Child Safety: GPS Child Locator," available online at *www.klaaskids.org/pg_gps_wherify.htm*.

8 Charles Layton, "The Information Squeeze," *American Journalism Review* (September 2002).

9 See, e.g., *www.cloudnet.com/~edrbsass/fdrlessons.htm*.

10 Marc Sandalow, "Bush Brands DUI Report 'Dirty Politics,'" *The San Francisco Chronicle* (November 4, 2000).

11 *Clinton v. Jones*, 520 U.S. 681 (1997); *United States v. Nixon*, 418 U.S. 683 (1974); "Referral to the United States House of Representatives Pursuant to Title 28, United States Code, §595(c), Submitted by The Office of the Independent Counsel, September 9, 1998," available online at *icreport.access.gpo.gov/report/1cover.htm.*

12 Ellen Goodman, "In This GE Divorce, Focus Isn't Wife's Greed," syndicated in *The Atlanta Journal–Constitution* (September 20, 2002); Kathy M. Kristof, "Welch Plans to Pay GE $2.5 Million a Year for Retirement Perks: Ex-Chairman Says Payments Were Proper," *The San Francisco Chronicle* (September 17, 2002).

13 Randy Shilts, *And The Band Played On: Politics, People, and the AIDS Epidemic*, St. Martin's Press, 1987, pp. 577, 588; Judith Serrin and William Serrin (eds.), *Muckraking!: The Journalism That Changed America*, The New Press, 2002, p. 76; *The San Francisco Chronicle*, July 25, 1985.

Counterpoint: Some Kinds of Information Should Always Be Protected

1 Eugene (Evgeny) Zamiatin, *We*, trans. Gregory Zilboorg, E.P. Dutton & Co., 1952. First published in English in 1924.

2 Amitai Etzioni, *The Limits of Privacy*, Perseus Books Group/Basic Books, 1999, pp. 64–67.

3 *Ibid.*, pp. 73–74.

4 Jamie Wilson, "Girl to Get Tracker Implant to Ease Parents' Fears," *Guardian Unlimited* (September 3, 2002).

5 Anita L. Allen, "Gender and Privacy," *Stanford Law Review* 52(2000): 1188–1190.

6 Mike Kiley, "Sammy Calls It Foul," *The Chicago Sun–Times* (June 30, 2002).

7 Jay Mariotti, "SI's Reilly Wonders If Sosa Is Clean," *The Chicago Sun–Times* (July 2, 2002).

8 C.W. Nevius, "Want Simple Answers? Find Simpler Problems." *The San Francisco Chronicle* (July 15, 2002).

9 Richard H. Rovere, *Senator Joe McCarthy*, World Publishing Company/Meridian, 1969; Victor Navasky, *Naming Names*, Penguin, 1981. For a defense of the hearings, see Whittaker Chambers, *Witness*, Random House, 1952. On the spying history, see Allen Weinstein and Alexander Vassiliev, *The Haunted Wood: Soviet Espionage in America: The Stalin Era*, Modern Library, 2000.

10 *NAACP v. Alabama*, 357 U.S. 449 (1958).

11 *Griswold v. Connecticut*, 381 U.S. 479, 483 (1965).

12 Katha Pollitt, "Slut Patrol," *The Nation* (September 30, 2002):10.

13 Robert Shelton, *No Direction Home: The Life and Music of Bob Dylan*, Ballantine, 1992, pp. 471–472.

14 Jan McGirk, "How Buffy's Secret Wedding Bewitched the Paparazzi," *The Independent* (September 7, 2002), available online at *news.independent.co.uk/world/americas/story.jsp?story=331164.*

15 Edward Guthmann, "Jason Gould Turns Camera On Himself: 'Inside Out' Explores Perils Faced by Children of Celebrities," *The San Francisco Chronicle* (December 10, 2000).

16 Restatement (2nd) of the Law of Torts, §652.

17 *Ibid.*, §652E and comments.

18 Deb Price, "Gerald Ford: Treat Gay Couples Equally," *The Detroit News* (October 29, 2001).

19 Gene Goodwin and Ron F. Smith, *Groping for Ethics in Journalism*, 3d ed., Iowa State University Press, 1994, pp. 255–256; *Sipple v. Chronicle Publishing Co.*, 154 Cal. App. 3d 1040 (Cal. 1st Dist., 1984); *Sipple v. Des Moines Register & Tribune Co.*, 82 Cal.App.3d 143 (Cal. 1st Dist., 1978).

20 The family break ruined Sipple's life. He died at 47 years of age.

Drawing Lines

1 *Griswold v. Connecticut*, 381 U.S. 479 (1965).

2 *Skinner v. Oklahoma*, 316 U.S. 535 (1942); *Loving v. Virginia*, 388 U.S. 1 (1967); *Eisenstadt v. Baird*, 405 U.S. 438 (1972); *Roe v. Wade*, 410 U.S. 113 (1973); *Carey v. Population Services International*, 431 U.S. 678 (1977); *Moore v. City of East Cleveland*, 431 U.S. 816 (1977); *Zablocki v. Redhail*, 434 U.S. 374 (1978); *Bowers v. Hardwick*, 478 U.S. 186 (1986); *Planned Parenthood v. Casey*, 404 U.S. 833. And see generally "Developments in the Law: The Constitution and the Family," *Harvard Law Review* 93(1980):1156.

Policy and History Research Resources on the Internet

The Federal Trade Commission: "Privacy: What You Do Know Can Protect You"
www.ftc.gov/bcp/conline/pubs/alerts/privprotalrt.htm
A "consumer alert" that offers links and addresses useful in reducing corporate privacy violations.

The Michigan State Attorney General: Consumer Alert: "Who Left the Cookies in the Cyberjar?"
www.ag.state.mi.us/cp/alerts/c_alerts/consumer_alert36.htm
Offers advice on rejecting and controlling "cookies." On cookies, what they do, and how to disable them, see also *www.junkbusters.com/cookies.html* and *www.epic.org/ privacy/internet/cookies/*. There are many cookie deletion/management programs available online, of varying safety and reliability, including some freeware.

The State of Maine: Department of the Secretary of State: "Protect Your Privacy & Prevent Identity Fraud"
www.state.me.us/sos/IDfraud.htm
A useful state-sponsored site on credit ratings and combating identity fraud.

The FBI: The Freedom of Information Act: Electronic Reading Room
foia.fbi.gov/room.htm
Among other investigation material, provides the publicly released parts of many famous people's FBI files. Subjects include Lucille Ball, Cesar Chavez, Albert Einstein, William Faulkner, Malcolm X, Thomas Mann, and Eleanor Roosevelt.

U.S. Federal Trade Commission: Privacy Agenda
www.ftc.gov/opa/2001/10/privacyagenda.htm
Interesting results can be had on any consumer privacy issue through a search of *www.ftc.gov* and *www.searchgov.com*—the websites of state attorneys general, especially those who are mentioned on the FTC site as working on consumer protection projects.

The University of Missouri: The Freedom of Information Center
www.missouri.edu/~foiwww/laws.html
Provides a guide to freedom of information laws and some privacy laws and links to "A Citizen's Guide on Using the Freedom of Information Act and the Privacy Act of 1974 to Request Government Records," House Report No. 107–371, 107th Congress, Second Session, published March 12, 2002 by the House Committee on Government Reform. The guide is also available at *www.house.gov/reform/ reports.htm* and via *www.gpo.gov/congress/*.

The U.S. Government Printing Office
www.access.gpo.gov
This site's "GPO Access" section offers a huge online archive of federal publications, including newer congressional reports and federal laws and regulations. The "Library Services" section provides addresses of local GPO depository libraries that maintain varying collections of government documents for public review. (Academic and law libraries are the most likely to carry older congressional reports that are not yet online.)

Bureau of Justice Statistics: *Report of the National Task Force on Privacy, Technology, and Criminal Justice Information*
www.ojp.usdoj.gov/bjs/pub/pdf/rntfptcj.pdf
A report by the U.S. Justice Department's National Task Force on Privacy, Technology, and Criminal Justice Information, released in August of 2001, just before the September 11 attacks; discusses the collection, use, and release of criminal record information.

Cornell Law School: Legal Information Institute
www.law.cornell.edu
Offers searchable unofficial editions of state and federal laws and court cases. In the U.S. Code, the "Notes" page for each code section offers a look into the law's history, including links to the Library of Congress's bill tracking system (THOMAS), which in turn can help in finding *Congressional Record* transcripts of the debates that surrounded the law's creation.

The Center for Democracy and Technology
www.cdt.org/security/usapatriot/hearings.shtml
Offers reports from a civil libertarian perspective on the current state of U.S. federal surveillance laws.

The American Civil Liberties Union (ACLU)
www.aclu.org
Campaigns for privacy rights and the constitutional rights of criminal defendants, immigrants, and other marginal groups. Its "Safe And Free" feature addresses some of the special constitutional concerns that have come up since the onset of the "war on terror."

Georgetown University: The Health Privacy Project
www.healthprivacy.org
This informative website includes texts of many useful articles and reports about health information privacy, especially on the Internet.

Harvard University: The Berkman Center for the Internet and Society: "Privacy in Cyberspace"
eon.law.harvard.edu/privacy
Offers online course materials prepared in 2002, including many selected readings on online privacy issues.

Other Online Resources

- On wiretapping issues, the following materials, all available on the Internet, may be of use: James X. Dempsey, "Communications Privacy in the Digital Age: Revitalizing the Federal Wiretap Laws to Enhance Privacy," *Albany Law Journal of Science & Technology* 8:1(1997), reprinted at *www.cdt.org/publications/lawreview/1997albany.shtml*; witnesses' prepared statements,

"The Fourth Amendment and the Internet," hearing before the United States House of Representatives, Subcommittee on the Constitution of the Committee on the Judiciary (July 24, 2000), available at *www.house.gov/ judiciary/con07241.htm*; "The 'Carnivore' Controversy: Electronic Surveillance and Privacy in the Digital Age," S. Hrg. 106–1057, Committee on the Judiciary, United States Senate, September 6, 2000, available via *www.gpo.gov/congress/*.

- The Electronic Privacy Information Center (*www.epic.org*), the Center for Democracy and Technology (*www.cdt.org*), Computer Professionals for Social Responsibility (*www.cpsr.org*) and the American Library Association (*www.ala.org/alaorg/oif/issues.html*), all generally liberal, have large collections of position papers and legal explanations on privacy issues. EPIC's topics include a section on student privacy, available at *www.epic.org/privacy/student/*.

- "The Dangers of Domestic Spying by Federal Law Enforcement: A Case Study on FBI Surveillance of Dr. Martin Luther King," is available from the ACLU at *www.aclu.org/congress/mlkreport.PDF*. It is a summary of part of the 1976 Church Committee Report cited in the text, with modern annotations discussing the problems of security and civil liberties in the wake of the September 11 attack.

- On the Japanese American Internment, see the Supreme Court cases of *Minoru Yasui v. United States*, 320 U.S. 115 (1943); *Kiyoshi Hirabayashi v. United States*, 320 U.S. 81 (1943); *Toyosaburo Korematsu v. United States*, 323 U.S. 214 (1944); *Ex Parte Mitsuye Endo*, 323 U.S. 283 (1944). On the 1980s *coram nobis* fight to reconsider these wartime cases, see Emil Guillermo, "Dangerous Talk," *The San Francisco Chronicle* (July 30, 2002).

- David Brin, whose book *The Transparent Society* is discussed in the text, has a personal website with comments on privacy and current events as well as promotion for his science-fiction books, at *www.kithrup.com/brin/*.

Useful Books

Brin, David. *The Transparent Society*. Addison-Wesley, 1998. Advances the arguments that there is no longer any point trying to preserve privacy and therefore the best goal is "transparency"—a world in which all players, including powerful institutions, are open to public scrutiny.

Chambers, Whittaker. *Witness.* Random House, 1952. Probably the classic argument that the famous Congressional hearings truly helped combat Soviet spying. On post–Cold War disclosures about espionage in that period, including material that suggests that Chambers was right, see Allen Weinstein and Alexander Vassiliev's *The Haunted Wood: Soviet Espionage in America—The Stalin Era* (Modern Library, 2000). On excesses of domestic spying from 1956 to 1971, see the "Church Committee Report," especially volume III. Formally this is known as the Report of the Senate Select Committee to Study Governmental Operations with Respect to Intelligence Activities, 94th Cong., 2d Sess., Rept. No. 94–755 (1976).

Etzioni, Amitai. *The Limits of Privacy.* Perseus/Basic Books, 1999. Etzioni, a communitarian philosopher, discusses HIV testing, "Megan's Laws" on sex offenders, computer encryption, identity cards, and medical information privacy, all from a perspective that argues that individuals should sometimes give up rights for the good of the group.

Inada, Lawson Fusao, ed. *Only What We Could Carry: The Japanese American Internment Experience.* California Historical Society/Heyday Books, 2000

Israel, Jerold H., and Wayne R. LaFave. *Criminal Procedure: Constitutional Limitations: In a Nutshell,* 6th ed. West Group, 2001. A good plain-language guide to search and seizure law.

Levy, Leonard W. *Origins of the Bill of Rights.* Yale University Press, Nota Bene, 2001. A readable general history of the Constitution.

Maki, Michelle T., Harry H.L. Kitano, and S. Megan Berthold. *Achieving the Impossible Dream: How Japanese Americans Obtained Redress.* University of Illinois Press, 1999.

Rehnquist, William. *All the Laws But One: Civil Liberties in Wartime.* Knopf/Borzoi, 1998. This discussion by Supreme Court Justice William Rehnquist is partly sympathetic to the notion that civil rights are different during times of national threat.

Smith, James Morton. *Freedom's Fetters: The Alien and Sedition Laws and American Civil Liberties.* Cornell University Press, 1956, 1967.

Van Dyke, Jon M., and Melvin M. Sakurai. *Checklists for Searches and Seizures in Public Schools.* West Group, published annually. Provides up-to-date details on the legal rights of students in schools.

Legislation and Case Law

Yick Wo v. Hopkins, 118 U.S. 356 (1886)
Immigrants are protected by the Fourteenth Amendment as "persons." Currently interpreted to grant to immigrants generally the basic civil rights of citizens— depending on the formal status and practical extent of their connection to the U.S.

Weeks v. United States, 232 U.S. 383 (1914)
Affirmed that evidence obtained in violation of the defendant's Fourth Amendment rights could not be considered at trial.

Olmstead v. United States, 277 U.S. 438 (1928)
Official investigators' telephone eavesdropping does not affect Fourth Amendment rights if the agents do not physically intrude. (Now overruled.) Memorable dissenting opinion by Justice Brandeis.

Minoru Yasui v. United States, 320 U.S. 115 (1943); *Kiyoshi Hirabayashi v. United States,* 320 U.S. 81 (1943); *Toyosaburo Korematsu v. United States,* 323 U.S. 214 (1944); *Ex Parte Mitsuye Endo,* 323 U.S. 283 (1944)
These cases first justified the Japanese-American Internment, then ended Japanese-Americans' imprisonment but did not overturn the original decision. Reopenings of these cases in the 1980s brought vindication to some of the original parties.

NAACP v. Alabama, 357 U.S. 449 (1958)
In the tense early days of the southern Civil Rights Movement, the Supreme Court held the National Association for the Advancement of Colored People did not have to violate its members' First Amendment free association rights—which are a kind of privacy rights—by disclosing their names to an Alabama court.

Mapp v. Ohio, 367 U.S. 643 (1961)
By the operation of the Fourteenth Amendment's Due Process Clause, the "Exclusionary Rule" that keeps improperly seized evidence out of court applies to evidence seized by any federal, state, or local official anywhere in the United States.

Griswold v. Connecticut, 381 U.S. 479 (1965)
Found that Connecticut officials violated individual privacy rights by trying to stop married couples from obtaining medical help to avoid pregnancy. Justice Douglas' opinion said marital privacy was one of several privacy rights implied in the Bill of Rights. Building on *Griswold*, subsequent cases have extended privacy protections to cover many aspects of family formation, including the right to abortion.

The Freedom of Information Act (1966)
First passed as Public Law 89–554, multiply amended since. Codified at 5 U.S.C. §552. FOIA creates a presumption that any federal document is available to the public unless the government can show why it should not be. It provides simple procedures allowing Americans to request copies of public documents and, among other provisions, requires government agencies to respond promptly.

Loving v. Virginia, 388 U.S. 1 (1967)
Affirmed the right of interracial couples to marry.

Katz v. United States, 389 U.S. 347 (1967)
Overturned *Olmstead:* "The Fourth Amendment protects people, not places."
Found that a suspect placing a call from a phone booth has a "reasonable
expectation of privacy" that may not be violated without a warrant.

The Omnibus Crime Control and Safe Streets Act of 1968 (Public Law 90–351)
Title III of this major legal overhaul created the foundations for the present-day
federal wiretapping process.

Terry v. Ohio, 392 U.S. 1 (1968)
Within limits, officers may stop, pat-search, and question a person who is behaving
suspiciously but not obviously breaking any law.

Eisenstadt v. Baird, 405 U.S. 438 (1972) and *Carey v. Population Services
International,* 431 U.S. 678 (1977)
Upheld the rights to sell contraceptives to unmarried people and to distribute
contraceptives to minors.

Roe v. Wade, 410 U.S. 113 (1973) and *Planned Parenthood v. Casey,*
505 U.S. 833 (1992)
Roe established the right to abortion as a privacy right, in a legal
argument that built on *Griswold v. Connecticut. Casey* is currently the
most important of several Supreme Court decisions since *Roe* that have
allowed legislators to restrict abortion in various ways so long as they
do not stop it entirely.

The Privacy Act of 1974
First passed as Public Law 93–579, current version codified at 5 U.S.C. §552a.
Entitles members of the public to request copies of government records
about themselves.

The Family Educational Records Privacy Act of 1974 (FERPA, Public Law
93–380, Title V), 20 U.S.C. §1232g *et seq.;* 34 CFR Part 99
Protects students' records against disclosure to outsiders, though there are
many exceptions. Allows students—or the parents of students under 18 years
of age—to challenge material in their records that they find unfair, and to
refuse to answer some kinds of intrusive surveys.

Tarasoff v. Regents of University of California, 17 Cal.3d 425 (1976)
This California holding, widely but not universally adopted in other states,
declared that therapists must "exercise reasonable care" to protect potential
victims if their patients threaten to do harm, even if this means disclosing
statements made during confidential therapy sessions.

The Foreign Intelligence Surveillance Act of 1978 (Public Law 95–511)
Created a parallel warrant procedure to make surveillance permissions easier
to get, from a special secret court, when an investigation involves the national
security; intended to distinguish between ordinary domestic policing and cases
involving spying or terrorism. The Justice Department as of this writing had
recently received a federal appellate court's approval for investigative information
sharing in terrorism-related cases that critics said would break down this
distinction. Some of the most controversial provisions of the USA PATRIOT
Act are expansions of FISA authority.

New Jersey v. T.L.O., 469 U.S. 325 (1985)
Students do have Fourth Amendment rights against searches by public school
officials, but they have fewer rights than adults in the outside world. School
searches without warrant or full probable cause are legal if reasonable given the
circumstances and the amount of suspicion.

The Electronic Communications Privacy Act of 1986 (Public Law 99–508)
Broadened the provisions in Title III of the Omnibus Crime Control and Safe
Streets Act of 1968 to cover electronic communications in addition to traditional
telephones. It also created two kinds of eavesdropping standards: one for finding
out what calls take place, and another for finding out what was said. At the time of
writing, being adapted controversially for use on the Internet.

The Video Privacy Protection Act of 1988 (Public Law 100–618), 18
U.S.C. §2710
Video stores in most cases may tell only police what a customer rents; police must
have a warrant, grand jury subpoena, or court order.

Skinner v. Railway Labor Executives' Assn., 489 U.S. 602 (1989) and
Treasury Employees v. Von Raab, 489 U.S. 656 (1989)
Skinner allowed federal transportation regulators to require alcohol and
drug testing for railroad employees involved in accidents or safety violations;
Von Raab allowed the Customs Service to require drug tests from people
applying for work involving drug enforcement, guns, or government secrets.
These two cases opened the way for drug testing of people who are not
personally suspected of drug use but who belong to a category that is a
subject of suspicion or concern.

California v. Acevedo, 500 U.S. 565 (1991)
One of the many Supreme Court cases announcing exceptions to the warrant
requirement. Justice Scalia's concurring opinion listed some of the many
exceptions and went on to argue that the warrant requirement should be
replaced with a court's assessment of whether a search or arrest was "reasonable."
This has not happened by the time of writing, but officers are now able to make
many kinds of searches without first obtaining a magistrate's permission.

The Communications Assistance for Law Enforcement Act of 1994
(CALEA, Public Law 103–414)
Designed to assure that new telephone systems would not block law enforcement eavesdropping. Interpretation currently controversial.

The Driver's Privacy Protection Act of 1994 (Public Law 103–322, Title XXX, §300001), 18 U.S.C. §2721 *et seq.*
Prohibited motor vehicle departments from releasing personal information out of driver's license files except for a few specified reasons, such as "matters of motor vehicle or driver safety and theft," and car manufacturers' product recalls.

Vernonia School Dist. 47J v. Acton, 515 U.S. 646 (1995)
The first case permitting random drug testing for public school students. Allowed an Oregon school district to impose drug testing on all high-school athletes.

The Health Insurance Portability and Accountability Act of 1996
(HIPAA) (Public Law 104–191)
Called for storing all U.S. health care information in a standardized, electronically movable format and created new privacy protections to compensate for the corresponding risks to privacy.

The Electronic Freedom of Information Act Amendments of 1996
("E-FOIA," Public Law 104–231), 5 U.S.C. §552
Strengthened the existing FOIA law requiring government agencies to release public records on request. Requires federal agencies to put frequently requested reports and decisions in online "reading rooms."

Clinton v. Jones, 520 U.S. 681 (1997); *United States v. Nixon,* 418 U.S. 683 (1974)
Found that even the President of the United States cannot stop or postpone a court case against him.

The Gramm-Leach-Bliley Act of 1999 (Public Law 106–102)
Banned some practices for gathering and sharing consumer financial information.

The USA PATRIOT Act (Public Law 107–56) and other antiterrorism laws passed after September 11, 2001
Among other provisions, PATRIOT permitted broader and more easily granted searches, including "roving wiretaps" that applied to any communications device used by a given person; undisclosed "sneak and peak" searches; and new authority to require information from businesses and institutions, such as hospitals and libraries. Created new, broader definitions of terrorism and helping terrorists.

Board of Education of Independent School District No. 92 of Pottawatomie County v. Earls, U.S. Supreme Court, June 27, 2002, Docket No. 01-332
Expanded the *Vernonia* decision about sports by endorsing a school policy in Tecumseh, Oklahoma that required all middle and high school students to agree to random drug testing before they could join extracurricular school activities.

Concepts and Standards

probable cause

expectation of privacy

the Fourth Amendment

warrant requirement

exceptions to the warrant requirement

privacy implied through many elements of the Bill of Rights

surveillance

personally identifiable information

transparency

panopticism

"invasion of privacy" torts

data mining

chilling effect

Beginning Legal Research

The goal of POINT/COUNTERPOINT is not only to provide the reader with an introduction to a controversial issue affecting society, but also to encourage the reader to explore the issue more fully. This appendix, then, is meant to serve as a guide to the reader in researching the current state of the law as well as exploring some of the public-policy arguments as to why existing laws should be changed or new laws are needed.

Like many types of research, legal research has become much faster and more accessible with the invention of the Internet. This appendix discusses some of the best starting points, but of course "surfing the Net" will uncover endless additional sources of information—some more reliable than others. Some important sources of law are not yet available on the Internet, but these can generally be found at the larger public and university libraries. Librarians usually are happy to point patrons in the right direction.

The most important source of law in the United States is the Constitution. Originally enacted in 1787, the Constitution outlines the structure of our federal government and sets limits on the types of laws that the federal government and state governments can pass. Through the centuries, a number of amendments have been added to or changed in the Constitution, most notably the first ten amendments, known collectively as the Bill of Rights, which guarantee important civil liberties. Each state also has its own constitution, many of which are similar to the U.S. Constitution. It is important to be familiar with the U.S. Constitution because so many of our laws are affected by its requirements. State constitutions often provide protections of individual rights that are even stronger than those set forth in the U.S. Constitution.

Within the guidelines of the U.S. Constitution, Congress—both the House of Representatives and the Senate—passes bills that are either vetoed or signed into law by the President. After the passage of the law, it becomes part of the United States Code, which is the official compilation of federal laws. The state legislatures use a similar process, in which bills become law when signed by the state's governor. Each state has its own official set of laws, some of which are published by the state and some of which are published by commercial publishers. The U.S. Code and the state codes are an important source of legal research; generally, legislators make efforts to make the language of the law as clear as possible.

However, reading the text of a federal or state law generally provides only part of the picture. In the American system of government, after the

106

legislature passes laws and the executive (U.S. President or state governor) signs them, it is up to the judicial branch of the government, the court system, to interpret the laws and decide whether they violate any provision of the Constitution. At the state level, each state's supreme court has the ultimate authority in determining what a law means and whether or not it violates the state constitution. However, the federal courts—headed by the U.S. Supreme Court—can review state laws and court decisions to determine whether they violate federal laws or the U.S. Constitution. For example, a state court may find that a particular criminal law is valid under the state's constitution, but a federal court may then review the state court's decision and determine that the law is invalid under the U.S. Constitution.

It is important, then, to read court decisions when doing legal research. The Constitution uses language that is intentionally very general—for example, prohibiting "unreasonable searches and seizures"—and court cases often provide more guidance. For example, the U.S. Supreme Court's 2001 decision in *Kyllo v. United States* held that scanning the outside of a person's house using a heat sensor to determine whether the person is growing marijuana is unreasonable—*if* it is done without a search warrant secured from a judge. Supreme Court decisions provide the most definitive explanation of the law of the land, and it is therefore important to include these in research. Often, when the Supreme Court has not decided a case on a particular issue, a decision by a federal appeals court or a state supreme court can provide guidance; but just as laws and constitutions can vary from state to state, so can federal courts be split on a particular interpretation of federal law or the U.S. Constitution. For example, federal appeals courts in Louisiana and California may reach opposite conclusions in similar cases.

Lawyers and courts refer to statutes and court decisions through a formal system of citations. Use of these citations reveals which court made the decision (or which legislature passed the statute) and when and enables the reader to locate the statute or court case quickly in a law library. For example, the legendary Supreme Court case *Brown v. Board of Education* has the legal citation 347 U.S. 483 (1954). At a law library, this 1954 decision can be found on page 483 of volume 347 of the U.S. Reports, the official collection of the Supreme Court's decisions. Citations can also be helpful in locating court cases on the Internet.

Understanding the current state of the law leads only to a partial understanding of the issues covered by the POINT/COUNTERPOINT series. For a fuller understanding of the issues, it is necessary to look at public-policy arguments that the current state of the law is not adequately addressing the issue. Many groups lobby for new legislation or changes to existing legislation; the National Rifle Association (NRA), for example, lobbies Congress and the state legislatures constantly to make existing gun control laws less restrictive and not to pass additional laws. The NRA and other groups dedicated to various causes might also intervene in pending court cases: a group such as Planned Parenthood might file a brief *amicus curiae* (as "a friend of the court")—called an "amicus brief"—in a lawsuit that could affect abortion rights. Interest groups also use the media to influence public opinion, issuing press releases and frequently appearing in interviews on news programs and talk shows. The books in POINT/COUNTERPOINT list some of the interest groups that are active in the issue at hand, but in each case there are countless other groups working at the local, state, and national levels. It is important to read everything with a critical eye, for sometimes interest groups present information in a way that can be read only to their advantage. The informed reader must always look for bias.

Finding sources of legal information on the Internet is relatively simple thanks to "portal" sites such as FindLaw (*www.findlaw.com*), which provides access to a variety of constitutions, statutes, court opinions, law review articles, news articles, and other resources—including all Supreme Court decisions issued since 1893. Other useful sources of information include the U.S. Government Printing Office (*www.gpo.gov*), which contains a complete copy of the U.S. Code, and the Library of Congress's THOMAS system (*thomas.loc.gov*), which offers access to bills pending before Congress as well as recently passed laws. Of course, the Internet changes every second of every day, so it is best to do some independent searching. Most cases, studies, and opinions that are cited or referred to in public debate can be found online—and *everything* can be found in one library or another.

The Internet can provide a basic understanding of most important legal issues, but not all sources can be found there. To find some documents it is necessary to visit the law library of a university or a public law library; some cities have public law libraries, and many library systems keep legal documents at the main branch. On the following page are some common citation forms.

COMMON CITATION FORMS

Source of Law	Sample Citation	Notes
U.S. Supreme Court	*Employment Division v. Smith*, 485 U.S. 660 (1988)	The U.S. Reports is the official record of Supreme Court decisions. There is also an unofficial Supreme Court ("S.Ct.") reporter.
U.S. Court of Appeals	*United States v. Lambert*, 695 F.2d 536 (11th Cir.1983)	Appellate cases appear in the Federal Reporter, designated by "F." The 11th Circuit has jurisdiction in Alabama, Florida, and Georgia.
U.S. District Court	*Carillon Importers, Ltd. v. Frank Pesce Group, Inc.,* 913 F.Supp. 1559 (S.D.Fla.1996)	Federal trial-level decisions are reported in the Federal Supplement ("F.Supp."). Some states have multiple federal districts; this case originated in the Southern District of Florida.
U.S. Code	Thomas Jefferson Commemoration Commission Act, 36 U.S.C., §149 (2002)	Sometimes the popular names of legislation—names with which the public may be familiar—are included with the U.S. Code citation.
State Supreme Court	*Sterling v. Cupp*, 290 Ore. 611, 614, 625 P.2d 123, 126 (1981)	The Oregon Supreme Court decision is reported in both the state's reporter and the Pacific regional reporter.
State statute	Pennsylvania Abortion Control Act of 1982, 18 Pa. Cons. Stat. 3203-3220 (1990)	States use many different citation formats for their statutes.

111

MARTHA A. BRIDEGAM studied at Harvard University and Hastings College of the Law and is a journalist and poverty lawyer. She has contributed to magazines including *The Baffler* and *Bad Subjects* and writes regularly on housing regulatory issues. Long-term projects include a landscape history of a site related to the Japanese American Internment. She maintains a serious amateur interest in the life and work of George Orwell and is a card-carrying member of the ACLU.

ALAN MARZILLI, of Durham, North Carolina, is an independent consultant working on several ongoing projects for state and federal government agencies and nonprofit organizations. He has spoken about mental health issues in over twenty states, the District of Columbia, and Puerto Rico; his work includes training mental health administrators, nonprofit management and staff, and people with mental illness and their family members on a wide variety of topics, including effective advocacy, community-based mental health services, and housing. He has written several handbooks and training curricula that are used nationally. He managed statewide and national mental health advocacy programs and worked for several public interest lobbying organizations in Washington, D.C. while studying law at Georgetown University.